WHALE

WHALE

THE ILLUSTRATED BIOGRAPHY

ASHA DE VOS

Illustrations by Adam Hook

Princeton University Press
Princeton and Oxford

CONTENTS

Published by Princeton University Press
41 William Street, Princeton, New Jersey 08540
99 Banbury Road, Oxford OX2 6JX
prcss.princeton.edu

GPSR Authorized Representative: Easy Access System Europe
Mustamäe tee 50, 10621 Tallinn, Estonia,
gpsr.requests@easproject.com

Library of Congress Control Number 2025930830

ISBN: 978-0-691-27321-1

Ebook ISBN: 978-0-691-27322-8

Typeset in Baskerville

Printed and bound in Malaysia
1 3 5 7 9 10 8 6 4 2

British Library Cataloging-in-Publication
Data is available

This book was conceived, designed, and produced by
UniPress Books Limited
Publisher: Jason Hook
Art direction: Alexandre Coco
Design: Paul Palmer-Edwards
Illustrator: Adam Hook

Cover design: Paul Palmer-Edwards
Cover images: Adam Hook

To Amma and Thaththa.

You gave me the sun, moon, stars, and, most importantly, the sea when you told me there were no boundaries to my life. You showed courage and confidence in my ability to find and create a path that most others thought was madness. I stand here as a testament to everything you both are.

To you, I owe Everything.

PREFACE

Writing a book is never easy and this one was particularly hard—although not for the reasons you might think. I ventured down a veritable rabbit hole of research in order to bring this incredible, multi-world-record-holding species to life. Blue Whales are the biggest animal Earth has ever known. They have the greatest appetite, they give birth to the largest babies, and they have the largest tongues, lungs, and hearts. Humpbacks have the longest appendages (their flippers) and sperm whales the biggest brains and loudest voices. Male Right Whales have the biggest testicles and Cuvier's Beaked Whales dive the deepest and hold their breath the longest. Orcas sit comfortably at the top of the marine food web, beating even great white sharks. The list of records feels endless, and as we continue to unravel more about the mysterious lives of whales, we can be sure that many others will follow.

A CUVIER'S BEAKED WHALE
These otherworldly creatures hold the world record for the deepest dives and longest breath holds.

I struggled to consolidate all the fascinating research and stories I have learnt and experienced in my more than two decades-long career observing and understanding these beasts. I made sure to feature the most up-to-date and interesting research, yet every day a new story appears that would be well worth including, and by this measure, no book can ever be truly complete. But I like to think that if I could speak to whales, they would agree that what you see on these pages is what they want to be known for. I spent months at my desk or curled up on my bean bag, poring over my notes, loving every second of the process and this opportunity to venture into the secret lives of the species I have worked with for so long. In some ways, this book felt like a beautiful escape from the madness and demands of the rest of my work. I am so excited for everyone to fall in love with whales, not just because they are charismatic and beautiful, but because of all they are on the inside too—from their astonishing anatomy to their surprisingly considerate cultures and even their moral values. There is much we can learn from them.

This book is designed to take you through the lives of these leviathans. We begin in Chapter 1 by meeting the family and learning how whales first came to be. We then move to Chapter 2 to explore how we study whales, and the tools and tricks that have given us so much insight (and yet still not enough) into their elusive lives. Chapter 3 looks at what makes a whale a whale, describing its anatomy and special adaptations that allow the animal to live its watery life successfully. Chapter 4 takes us to the beginning of a little whale or whale calf's life, and even before that, as we talk about birth, conception, and the joys of motherhood in whales. Chapter 5 looks at everything from mating to menopause and its importance, as well as whales' family lives and the contrasting ways of living. Chapter 6 is important as it looks at all the different feeding and hunting behaviors and techniques, and considers how a single species might vary its tactics in different oceans and maintain efficiency while finding its food. Migration, driven by the need to find food and mates, is at the core of Chapter 7. Chapter 8 covers the most characteristic features of whales, including the haunting and complex songs of the Humpbacks, the clicks of Sperm Whales, and exactly how these species navigate the world using sound rather than sight.

Chapter 9 is a grand celebration of humanity's long relationship with whales, from our most negative interactions to the most positive ones, and finally, in Chapter 10 we look at the importance of whale populations to our planet, the importance of protecting them from the threats they face, and the efforts being made by selfless individuals to bring whales back from the brink.

This book was a challenge, but also a true joy to write. I hope you feel this joy emanating through the pages and that you will learn lots about one of the most fascinating species ever to have roamed our planet.

1

MEET THE FAMILY

AN INTRODUCTION

WHALES 101

Every good story starts with an introduction to the family, and in this story, knowing who we are talking about is key to following the plot. Welcome to the watery world of whales and dolphins. Whales and dolphins belong to the class Mammalia, where they sit comfortably among a range of mammals that live on land—from the elephant to the shrew. Being marine dwellers, they are clumped with a few other marine mammals you might expect, including seals and sea lions, and at least one that might surprise you—the polar bear (*Ursus maritimus*). But whales, dolphins, and porpoises soon break away and form their own order—Cetacea.

There are approximately 90 species within the order Cetacea, which exhibit a 2,200-fold increase in body mass from the smallest species, the 8–9-st Vaquita (*Phocoena sinus*), to the largest, the up to 32,000-st Blue Whale (*Balaenoptera musculus*). Cetaceans separated about 30 million years ago (MYA) into two groups with different feeding strategies. If they use baleen—large comb-like structures made of keratin—to filter feed, they fall into the suborder Mysticeti, which is home to all of the baleen whales, known (appropriately enough) as the mustached whales. Those that use teeth to catch or consume prey can be found in the suborder Odontoceti, known as toothed whales. Each of these suborders hosts several families in which similar species are clustered together.

While these terms are sometimes hard to remember, key physical characteristics allow us to recognize and differentiate between baleen whales and toothed whales. Of course, their feeding structures would be a good place to start, but for most people whose time with a whale is spent sitting on a boat, they may not be the first thing seen, so relying on a feature easily spotted as soon as the whales rise to the surface makes more sense. This brings us to blowholes. Baleen whales have two blowholes, while toothed whales have just one. Typically, they are slap bang in the center of their head, but Sperm Whales (*Physeter macrocephalus*), as always, like to be different. They have evolved such that their blowhole is positioned on the top left of their nose, so that every time they blow or exhale, the vapor emerges at an angle—this makes it easy to recognize them from a distance.

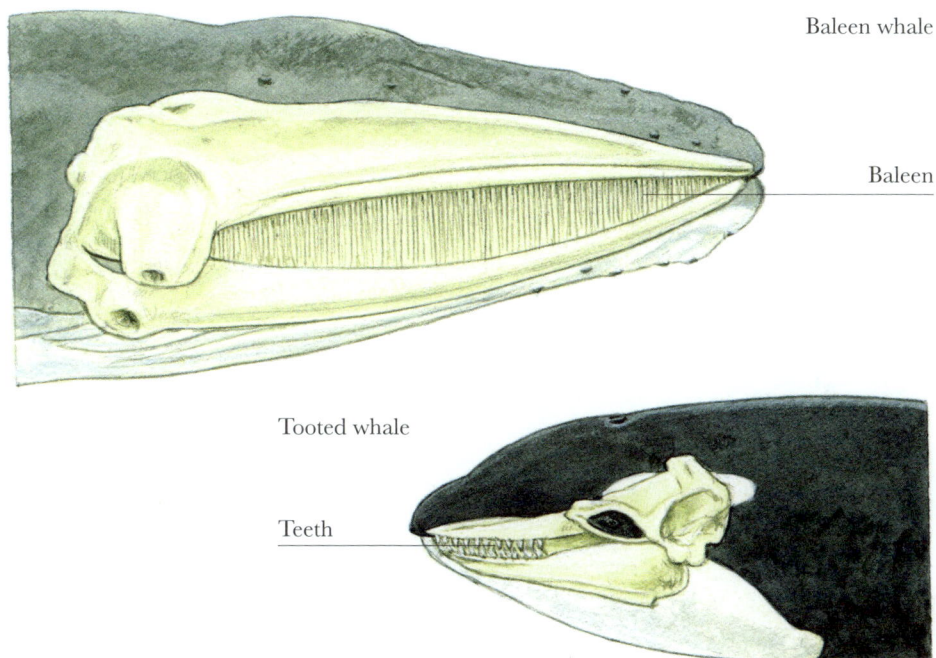

Baleen whale

Baleen

Tooted whale

Teeth

BALEEN V. TOOTHED WHALES
All whales fit into one of these two categories, based on how they feed.

A feature of toothed whales that can't be seen is that they use echolocation to find their food. Like bats, they emit a series of "clicks" that hit their prey and bounce right back to them, where they are perceived by their lower jaw, which is filled with a fatty fluid. From there, the acoustic information is transmitted to the middle ear and ultimately to the brain for interpretation. It's remarkable to think that the whales can emit the clicks and process the information coming back at them all while moving toward their prey.

On the other hand, despite an innate ability to locate swarms of tiny prey in a vast ocean, the secret of baleen whale food sourcing is still not completely understood. Scientists believe they use light for finding food, and Blue Whales in particular have large eyes (11 inches or 4.3 cm in diameter) that allow them

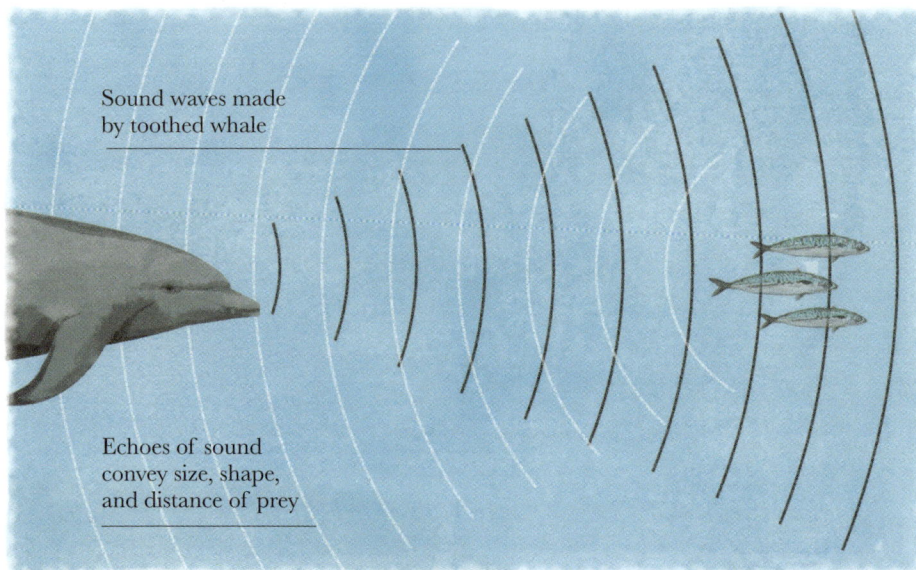

Sound waves made by toothed whale

Echoes of sound convey size, shape, and distance of prey

ECHOLOCATION
Toothed whales use echolocation to find prey and avoid obstacles.

to gather more light at depth. They may also listen to their prey or use tiny hairs on their chin, called *vibrissae*, to feel their way through the world—or their prey when they swim into a swarm. Their memory also plays a role, because rorquals—the largest group of baleen whales, which includes Blue, Fin (*Balaenoptera physalus*), Sei (*Balaenoptera borealis*), and Humpback Whales (*Megaptera novaeangliae*), and the two species of Minke Whale (*Balaenoptera acutorostrata, B. bonaerensis*)—are known to return to feeding areas that have provided successful feeding opportunities in previous years. Knowing how baleen whales track and find their food is important, as it can help scientists predict where they might go to feed, enabling better management of human activities in those crucial areas.

In case you are thinking that I will mention porpoises once, fleetingly, and then forget to tell you more, think again. Porpoises, like dolphins, are toothed whales, but there are important differences on closer inspection. Dolphins typically have more elongated and streamlined bodies than porpoises, with a pronounced beak, or rostrum. They also tend to be larger than their cousins, which have rounded faces and no distinct beaks. Dolphin dorsal fins are more curved, while porpoises have triangular, upright dorsal fins. Interestingly, their teeth are shaped differently, with dolphins having conically shaped teeth and porpoises having flatter, spade-shaped teeth.

Other toothed whales, Orca (*Orcinus orca*), False Killer Whale (*Pseudorca crassidens*), and Pilot Whales (*Globicephala macrorhynchus, G. melas*), and all those other curiously shaped marine-dwelling cetaceans with teeth are, in fact, separated only superficially. It is because they are so closely related that we can refer to all cetaceans as whales as their stories unfold on the pages of this book.

Dolphin

Curved, pointy fin

Longer beak (rostrum)

Pointy, cone-shaped teeth

Porpoise

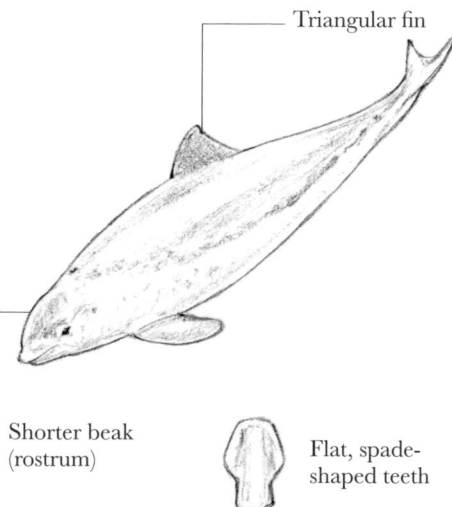

Triangular fin

Shorter beak (rostrum)

Flat, spade-shaped teeth

DOLPHINS AND PORPOISES
At a glance they may appear similar, but important differences distinguish these two animals.

THE EVOLUTIONARY HISTORY OF WHALES

Now that we know how to broadly tell them apart, it's perhaps pertinent to ask where whales come from: What are their evolutionary origins? It is probably no surprise to learn that the closest living relatives (or sister group) of whales are the hippopotamuses, given they share several adaptations to life in a watery world, including possessing oil-producing skin glands, lacking hair, and using underwater vocalizations for communication. However, this does not make them the ancestors of whales, and their large size and aquatic affinity evolved separately from whales. While the first hippos evolved from their ancient relatives, called anthracotheres, 15 MYA, the first whales evolved over 50 MYA—the ancestors of both were terrestrial. This shift from land to water was a transition that entailed major physiological and morphological changes.

There are many branches in the evolutionary tree of whales, but the most important one is the emergence of *Pakicetus*, often considered the first whale. With a long skull, large teeth, limbs designed for walking, no tail flukes, and nostrils far forward, it looked more like a wolf than a whale. However, the key giveaway is the inner-ear region, which is surrounded by a bony wall called the involucrum and resembles those of living whales—it is unlike any other mammal's. Next, we have *Ambulocetus*, an alligator-like creature with paddle-shaped hands and feet and a long, muscular tail. By studying the isotopes of oxygen in fossil bones, scientists have found that *Ambulocetus* had already taken the plunge (pun intended, of course) into the aquatic realm, drinking both salt and fresh water and likely living in estuaries or bays—midway between fresh water and open ocean. It even had a fat pad in the jaw used for hearing, much like modern-day toothed whales. Skip forward to the *Dorudon*, and we have a completely aquatic beast with nostrils shifted further back, tail flukes, and very small hind legs—akin to the whales we see today (which, interestingly, do have vestigial hind limbs, although these are not external).

Indohyus — Thick, bony wall around middle ear. Freshwater semi-aquatic habitat.

55 MYA

Pakicetus — Large, powerful tail, shorter legs, fat pad in jaw for hearing. Brackish water habitat.

50 MYA

Ambulocetus — Saltwater habitat.

45 MYA

Kutchicetus — Nasal opening shifted back. Eyes on the side of the head.

40 MYA

Rodhocetus — Tail fluke. Very small hind legs. Nasal opening shifted further back.

35 MYA

Dorudon — Complete loss of hind legs. Nasal opening reaches position of blowhole in living whales.

30 MYA

Odontocetes — Echolocation for hunting.

25 MYA

Mysticetes — Baleen for filtering food.

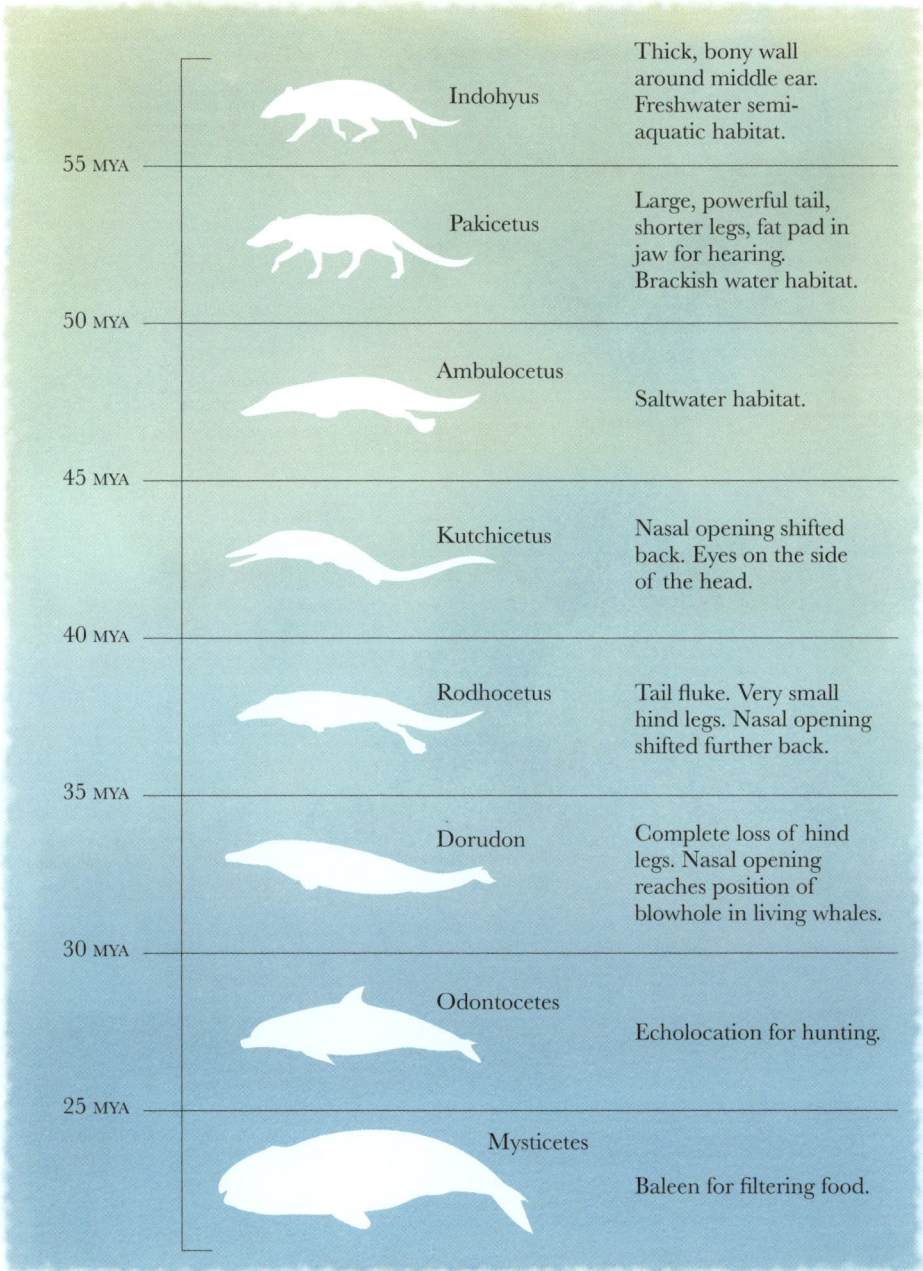

PHYLOGENY
Whale evolution.

Other evolutionary changes have included the increased use of the whole vertebral column in locomotion. Ancient aquatic whales evolved from land-dwelling, four-legged animals designed to run, with their limbs beneath them and flexible backbones that could bend up and down to extend their spine and stride. This resulted in horizontal tail flukes (fins)—unlike the vertical tail flukes of fish—because cetaceans only use the shorter muscles connected to the rear of the body and use their upper bodies for direction. Unlike living whales, their ancestors' elbow joints were flexible but could lock, allowing for better propulsion through the water. Of course, the hind limbs soon vanished. These skeletal changes were vital for transitioning to the fully aquatic lifestyle that modern whales enjoy today.

WHAT'S IN A NAME?

The extant populations of whales we encounter on forays to the ocean today are referred to fondly by names that are sometimes descriptive while at other times confusing. These names often come from an era gone by, generously provided by whalers. Let's start with the giant of our oceans, the Blue Whale. Despite what the name implies, these leviathans are not blue. Instead, their skin is a mottled gray color. This is even more confusing when you consider that Blue Whales are gigantic and hard to miss, and therefore, one would assume that their color patterns would be easy to see and describe. So why are they called "Blue Whales"? Blue Whales appear blue for the same reason the ocean is blue—thanks to a phenomenon called light scattering. Colors with a longer wavelength, like red, yellow, and green, are quickly absorbed in the upper layers of the water column, while blue, with its shorter wavelength, penetrates deeper, giving everything a blue hue. The same principle applies to the Blue Whale's skin and blubber, which scatter the shorter blue wavelengths of light more effectively, making the whale appear blue to our eyes when seen underwater or in certain light conditions. In many ways, this name is less confusing than the nineteenth-century name of "sulphur bottom" used by American whalers to describe their yellowish bellies—a result of the colonies of diatoms that sometimes reside on their undersides.

Sperm Whales, the largest toothed whales on the planet, have perhaps the most curious name of all. It is said that when whalers hunting these whales cut them up they were the first to find the enormous fluid-filled organ that makes up the bulk of a Sperm Whale's huge head. This organ, now called the *spermaceti organ* (formerly the *case*), contains a white liquid that the whalers thought was sperm. As it turns out, they were wrong. It was not sperm. We now know that the spermaceti organ is filled with an oil that helps the whales focus sound, particularly the powerful sound waves used for echolocation.

* * *

The name "Right Whale," on the other hand, is a haunting reminder of our brutal past and the violent history of these animals. They were so named because they were the "right" whale to hunt. Their slow, lumbering movements made them an easy catch; they would stay near the surface where they were easy to spot and follow, and, thanks to all their blubber, they floated when

A RIGHT WHALE
This simple name has surprisingly dark origins.

19

ORCA OR KILLER WHALE?
All cetaceans are carnivorous; it seems unfair that only Orcas get such a brutal epithet.

killed, making them easy to tow to shore. They were also the "right whales" to kill because the thick blubber of one whale yielded over 40 barrels of oil, which was sold as fuel for oil lamps, among other things.

This brings us to Bowhead Whales (*Balaena mysticetus*), considered the longest-living marine mammals (see Chapter 2). They also have the largest mouth and head in the animal kingdom, taking up about a third of their body length. Their upper jaw is arched upward, forming the bow-shaped head that gives them their name—and a permanent deep frown.

Killer Whales have perhaps got the worst deal of all. Their name automatically conjures up images of fierce hunters and makes them sound brutal, almost Jack the Ripper-esque. But that is not the whole truth. As it happens, they were called "whale killers" by sailors who witnessed them attacking cetaceans of a range of sizes. This name then gradually switched to "killer whale," which still does not completely reflect their true nature. While some feast on marine mammals, of all sizes, one ecotype (which means a population that is adapted to local environmental conditions) has no interest in large blubbery foods but instead indulges in a piscivorous diet comprising species like salmon. Sure, they also hunt and kill their fishy prey, but given that all cetaceans are carnivorous, it feels harsh to single them out. A lot of people also assume that the Killer Whales got their name because they kill humans. It is important to highlight that there have been no human deaths at the flippers of wild Killer Whales to date. And let us not forget that Killer Whales are actually dolphins, the largest in our oceans. To show this species some respect, we will call them Orcas for the remainder of this book.

WHERE ARE WHALES FOUND?

Now that we have met some of the key characters in this book, it is important to highlight that whales are a pretty cosmopolitan group and—whether we are referring to Blue Whales, Humpback Whales, or Orcas—their ranges extend over most of Earth's oceans. From the equator to the poles, they are found in shallow and deep water, and in cold and warm currents. In some cases, their

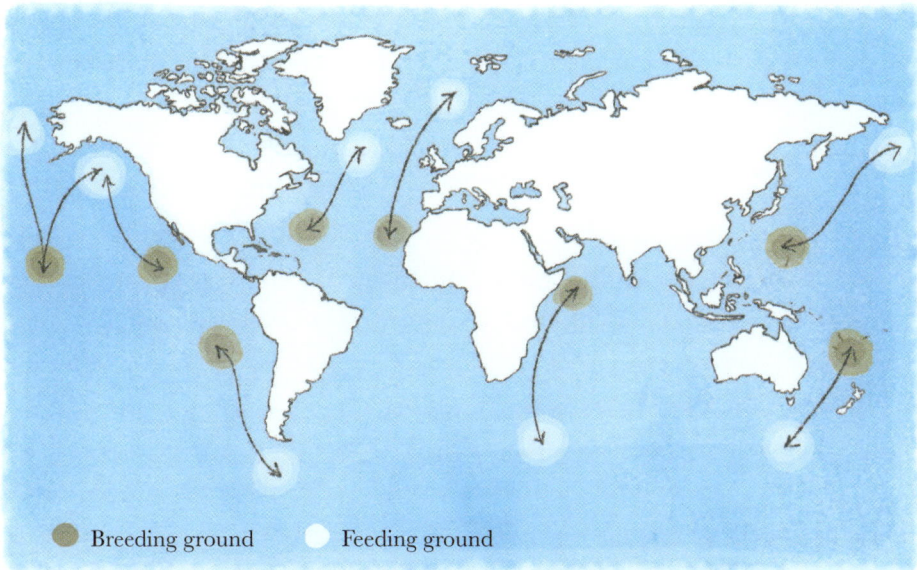

Breeding ground   Feeding ground

HUMPBACK WHALE MIGRATION ROUTES
Whales often travel vast distances between their breeding and feeding grounds.

smaller dolphin cousins can even be found venturing into brackish water lagoons and further inland in fresh water, including rivers.

Many whales feed in cold waters during the summer when there is an abundance of food, and spend the winter months in warmer waters, where they mate, give birth, and nurse their young. These whales are called *capital breeders* because they finance their reproduction using stored reserves. Species that undergo long migrations, including Humpback and Gray Whales (*Eschrichtius robustus*), feed voraciously on their colder feeding grounds and may not eat for the entirety of their migration to their breeding ground, where they will give birth and nurse before journeying back months later. Of course, not all whales migrate. The northern Indian Ocean population of Pygmy Blue Whales (*Balaenoptera musculus brevicauda*) spend their lives in the warm waters of this region, and Bryde's Whales (*Balaenoptera edeni*) remain exclusively in warm tropical waters too.

BEING SOCIAL

While baleen whales largely keep to themselves, their cousins the toothed whales are generally quite social creatures. They can be found in small- to medium-sized pods or, in the case of oceanic dolphins, in incredibly large pods, for short or long periods of time. While this is the norm, it is not the rule, because river dolphins often live solitary lives except when it is time to mate.

Social interactions of toothed whales largely fall into two groups: fission–fusion societies, which are more common among smaller whales, and matriarchal pods, which are more common among larger whales. As the term *fission–fusion* implies, in some species pods fuse to form groups of hundreds, sometimes thousands, that stick together for hours to days. After this period, they break up into subgroups and go their separate ways again. These fission–fusion societies are, therefore, inherently unstable. Matriarchal groups, on the other hand, are far more stable. Matriarchal groups organize around one or two key females,

SOCIAL GROUPS
A pod of Pilot Whales.

their female relatives, unrelated mates, and their offspring. These pods can be large, sometimes as big as 50 individuals, and female offspring remain with their birth pod for life. Some species, such as the Risso's Dolphins (*Grampus griseus*) around Terceira Island in the Azores, have a hybrid model where dolphins usually join up and separate as expected in a fission–fusion society, but at other times unrelated individuals travel together over long periods.

Regardless of the type of social interaction, this sociality allows for the transfer of vital information both vertically and horizontally through the pods, and enables individuals to be prepared for what's to come. Sperm Whales, perhaps the most social of all whale species, can be found in groups of 20–50 and, in rare cases, even 100. The biggest groups are often aggregations of matriarchal pods comprising grandmothers, mothers, and their offspring, which use the tropics throughout the year. Sometimes, these groups might also include a roving male. Unfortunately, being social means Sperm Whales gather in numbers in specific ocean areas, which made them highly vulnerable to whalers in the 1800s.

In a compelling example of the social transfer of information, in 1980

23

whale-watchers spotted a single Humpback Whale off the East Coast of the United States engaging in a modified version of bubble-net feeding (see Chapter 6 for details of feeding behaviors). Instead of just building a wall with bubbles, which is the done thing, the whale slapped the surface of the water with its tail before blowing bubbles. This behavior, called lobtailing, had never been seen in combination with bubble-net feeding before. The behavior caught on, and by 1989 many populations slapped the water before bubble-netting. This change in feeding behavior resulted from the ingenuity of the pioneer whale, which was driven to adjust its behavior by a reduction in the whales' favorite food, herring, resulting in a need to switch to a new prey species, sand lance (also known as sand eels). The biggest determinant of whether or not the behavior spread was whether an individual had watched another Humpback Whale engage in this new mode of feeding.

Advanced social behaviors, such as the ability to form tight-knit social groups and complex relationships, call each other by name—as in the case of Orcas—

LOBTAILING AND BUBBLE-NETTING
A distinctive feeding technique that spread through the Humpback population of the East coast of the U.S.

and use tools—as the *Tursiops aduncus* Bottlenose Dolphin is known to do—are a result of whales' anatomically sophisticated brains, specifically the expansion of the brain, known as *encephalization*. The idea that more social animals have larger brains relative to less social animals is a key idea behind the cultural brain hypothesis. This suggests that larger brains evolved in response to the demands of navigating complex social environments, which require enhanced cognitive abilities for social interaction, communication, and learning from others. This hypothesis emphasizes the roles of culture and social structures in shaping human intelligence and brain size.

Stories of the importance of social networks abound, from Risso's Dolphins to Bottlenose Dolphins and other species. Fundamentally, these stories serve as a reminder to us that social networks are important for the survival of whales.

STILL SO MUCH TO LEARN

Whales are some of the largest animals that have ever roamed our planet, and just when we think we have met them all, we realize we have not. Some recently discovered and renamed species provide insight into how much we still have to learn about these amazing beasts.

Rice's Whales (*Balaenoptera ricei*) look extremely like Bryde's Whales (*Balaenoptera edeni*), even down to the three prominent ridges on their heads—other species have just one. However, in 2021, based on their skull morphology and unique vocalizations, Rice's Whales were confirmed as a distinct species. Endemic to the Gulf of Mexico, they do not share a propensity for tropical and subtropical waters with Bryde's Whales. Rice's Whales are now critically endangered; fewer than 100 remain alive today. Conservation strategies must ensure the availability of their favorite prey, the silver-rag driftfish. Rice's Whales are picky eaters and choose this specific food because it is an energy-dense fish, chock full of proteins and lipids.

Omura's Whales (*Balaenoptera omurai*) were correctly classified for the first time as recently as 2003. Originally mistaken as a pygmy form of the Bryde's Whale, it was only in 2017 that the species was confirmed in Sri Lankan waters. I myself once nearly mistook an Omura for a Bryde's Whale; I was photographing an individual for an identification catalog when I saw some unusual white patches on its body. Fortunately, my photos allowed me to see that it was, in fact, an Omura's Whale. This species has now been recorded in all ocean basins, excluding the central and eastern Pacific.

Deraniyagala's Beaked Whale (*Mesoplodon hotaula*) is one of the least-studied marine mammals of our planet. Everything we knew about them was based on stranded specimens, until a probable live sighting in 2007 and five further sightings in the South China Sea between 2019 and 2023. More importantly, it took 51 years after the original discoverers' suspicions that it was a different species to be formally confirmed. In 1963, Dr. Deraniyagala described a nearly 15 ft long blue-gray beaked whale that stranded near Colombo as a new species, *Mesoplodon hotaula* (aptly, *hotaula* means pointed beak in the local language of Sinhala) or Deraniyagala's Beaked Whale. However, in 1965, biologists reclassified *Mesoplodon hotaula* as an existing species—the Ginkgo-Toothed Beaked Whale (*Mesoplodon ginkgodens*). In 2014, by using fragments of ancient DNA drilled out of the bones of stranded specimens, it was at last confirmed that while the Deraniyagala's Beaked Whale is closely related to the Gingko-Toothed Beaked Whale, it is indeed a separate species.

The Spade-Toothed Whale *(Mesoplodon traversii)*, considered the "rarest of the rare" whale species, was known from only 6 records over 150 years, until in 2024 a 16-ft specimen stranded in New Zealand (where all but one of the previous records were also made). Not only is this species an elusive deep diver, much like its cousins, but it also traverses the vast expanse of the under-studied Pacific Ocean. The dissection of the most recent specimen provided much fascinating insight into this species, including the fact that it has nine stomachs.

RIVER DOLPHINS

When someone says whale, most people think of Humpback Whales. When someone says dolphin, most people think of Bottlenose Dolphins. These species have dominated our screens and books, thanks to their tendency to be showy, well studied, and in the news. The sad truth is that river dolphins get little airtime because most people do not even know they exist, which is something we must change. It would be remiss to write a book about whales which did not detour into the less salty world of this nonetheless fascinating group.

Physical appearance

Six species of river dolphins roam some of the greatest river systems on our planet, specifically the Ayeyarwady, Ganges, Indus, Mekong, Mahakam, and Yangtze in Asia and the Amazon and Orinoco in South America. They are recognizable because they all possess some combination of a suite of common features—slender beaks lined with lots of teeth, small eyes, flexible necks and bodies, pronounced forehead melons, large flippers, and small, low dorsal fins.

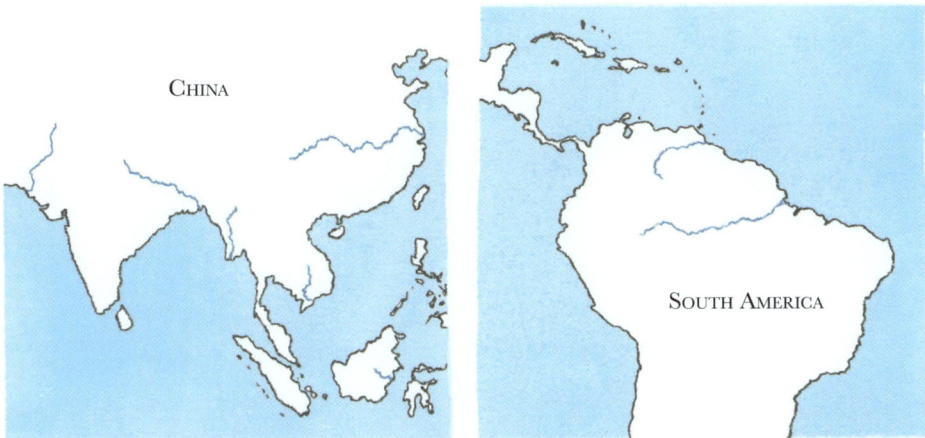

CHINA

SOUTH AMERICA

RIVER SYSTEMS
River dolphins are found in some of the greatest river systems across Asia and South America.

27

Unlike their ocean-dwelling cousins, who are often adorned with striped and spotted patterns, river dolphins are plainer, often sporting a solid brownish-gray palette with minimal patterning. Even the pink dolphins of the Amazon (*Inia geoffrensis*) are only so colorful because when they are active, the blood vessels in their skin dilate (sending blood to the skin, as it is the part of the body closest to the water) to regulate their body temperature, as opposed to pink being part of their default appearance. When inactive, these same dolphins return to their original grayish hue. That said, some older adult males may have permanent pink patches because of scar tissue formed during battles with one another. This rather drab natural colouration makes sense if you consider their favorite habitat—murky brown water with low visibility.

Research has shown that favorite foods are the primary determinant of a cetacean's face shape or skull morphology. Like river dolphins, those with longer snouts and many teeth are designed to catch small, fast prey like fish. (Shorter snouts are helpful if you are a suction feeder.) Amazon river dolphins use their snouts to stir up the bottom of the river and catch fish that hide there, while they use their hundreds of teeth to chew crunchy bony fish and crush turtles. River dolphin eyes are small, and in the case of the Ganges (*Platanista gangetica*) and Indus River (*Platanista minor*) dolphins, they are effectively blind, because sight is simply not very useful in turbid rivers thick with brown sediment washed down from the Himalayas upstream.

Feeding and navigation

Amazon River Dolphins do have good eyesight under water. However, like other river dolphins, they use echolocation to navigate and feed, which is why they have such bulbous melons on their foreheads. Many people are familiar with echolocation as bats and marine-dwelling toothed whales use it, but river dolphins tap into different frequencies and use different techniques that help them navigate their own unique environment. Given the need to navigate obstacles in rivers, flooded forests, and beneath floating vegetation, they have evolved a low dorsal fin, unlike the triangular one of their marine cousins, simply so that it does not get in the way. Their large flippers allow them to maneuver skillfully in this environment too. Flexible spines are characteristic of the slower-moving coastal, estuarine, and river dolphins, who tend to turn their heads from side to side when navigating and finding prey. In contrast, less flexible spines are part of the design of their faster, pelagic cousins.

Evolution

Amazingly, despite these many similarities between species, river dolphins are not universally related. The only thing they truly all have in common is their love for fresh water. In fact, river dolphins are a great example of convergent evolution. Based on fossil evidence, it is thought that between 11.6 and 16 MYA, marine dolphins repeatedly and in unrelated instances made their way into the shallow waters of what are now inland regions of South America, China, eastern and western India, and Pakistan. As sea levels then dropped, these individuals were trapped, leaving them river-bound. This new environment drove their independent speciation and specialization, which ultimately enabled them to survive in their new homes.

Uniquely, one species, the Franciscana Dolphin (*Pontoporia blainvillei*), first evolved into the river form and then returned to the sea. Today, it can be found cruising in estuaries and coastal waters across South America. Despite looking like a river dolphin on the outside, it apparently yearned for its ancestral state. Fransicana is the closest relative of the Boto, or Amazon River Dolphin, and the bigger counterpart to the smaller, gray Tucuxi (*Sotalia fluviatilis*). While Tucuxi are river dolphins, they look and leap out of the water more like their marine cousins.

The Indus and Ganges River Dolphins are also two distinct species, despite being erroneously lumped together in the past. While Ganges River Dolphins have a distinct protruding frontal bone behind the nasal opening, the Indus River Dolphin has a flat bone in the same location. Ganges River Dolphins also have fewer teeth. These distinct differences solidified the separation of the two species, even though both are found in South Asian river systems.

Aerial urination

Amazon River Dolphins swimming along the Tocantins River in Brazil have recently been caught on camera projectile urinating. The males roll onto their backs and urinate into the air, which is odd enough, but what's more, other males will then seek out the stream and position themselves under—or stick their snout precisely—where the urine comes back down to the water. Given the bristly nature of the Botos' snouts, perhaps they do this to decode messages locked in the urine. What messages, you might ask? Social cues related to physical health, group dominance, and perhaps even reproductive availability. While the idea of a dolphin peeing while swimming in linear, circular, or zigzag directions to communicate with other dolphins might sound weird, terrestrial animals use scent-marking all the time, and we seem to think that's fine.

Threats

Unfortunately, while these species have chosen to live in some of the world's greatest river systems, these same systems also support the lives of millions of people. As such, today all species of river dolphin are endangered, some critically so. This is due to habitat loss and fragmentation as a result of hydropower dams; sand mining and deforestation; pollution from agriculture, industry, and mining; vessel collisions; poorly managed tourism; and fishery interactions such as bycatch and direct takes. Since the 1980s, river dolphin populations have declined by nearly 73 percent.

In September and October 2023, the longest drought in the Amazon Rainforest's recorded history trapped some dolphins in extremely low water levels, which heated up to unbearable temperatures—reaching 102°F (39°C)—in Lake Tefé, a tributary of the Amazon in Amazonas, Brazil. This, along with the presence of various toxins and pollutants, resulted in a mass mortality event that killed about 330 Amazon Pink River Dolphins. The devastating impact of this on the already small and endangered population cannot be underestimated.

According to Brazilian folklore, pink dolphins emerge from the river on full moon nights as attractive men capable of conquering and impregnating young women before returning to the river. Therefore, children with unknown fathers are sometimes insultingly called "children of the dolphin." A colonial-era myth led to a false belief that perfumes or *pusangas* made from the body parts of river dolphins are potent love potions, creating a market for this species and leading to them being hunted and sold illegally. They are also killed when caught ripping open fishing nets to steal fish, and as recently as a decade or so ago, they were killed as bait to capture fish or as meat for human consumption. However, Amazonian communities deeply respect this species, even performing rituals to seek their permission before fishing in the river.

The first cetacean pronounced extinct in recent history is the Baiji, or Chinese River Dolphin (*Lipotes vexillifer*). Overfishing sadly robbed them of their prey and led to entanglements in fishing gear. The decline in their numbers happened fast, with thousands in the 1950s reducing to approximately 400 in the 1980s and dwindling to just a handful in the 1990s, until they were officially pronounced extinct in 2007. While efforts were made to protect this species by establishing protected areas, their tendency to follow migratory fish stocks up and down the river meant that static protection was futile. The last confirmed sighting and photographic evidence of the Baiji was in 2002.

In Pakistan, however, collective action has successfully doubled the local river dolphin population to up to 2,000 individuals. Similarly, numbers of the Yangtze Finless Porpoise (*Neophocaena asiaeorientalis*), the only freshwater porpoise in the world, increased by about 23 percent in the last five years to approximately 1,249. While these increases are positive, the population sizes remain small, and for species with slow reproductive cycles, any losses are significant.

While threats increase and populations decrease, it is important to remember that river dolphins, like their cousins, are important for the proper functioning of the ecosystem. Considered a sentinel species, their presence in waterways indicates a thriving ecosystem replete with food and favorable water quality for these species and all those around them. Their protection benefits the entire system.

2

HOW WE KNOW
WHAT WE KNOW
ABOUT WHALES

IN THE FLUKE-PRINTS OF GIANTS

In order to tell its story, you need to understand the life of a creature. But how do you gain an understanding of an animal whose life you witness only in fleeting moments? As a keen observer, you pay close attention, to discover what you can from the fragments of their lives you are privy to. And you innovate.

From discovering the size of the population to the details of whales' underwater lives, scientists learn from watching them. How we understand their world has much to do with how close they are to shore, and therefore how accessible they are to us, and the tools and methods we choose to help us gain our understanding. We take tiny samples of body tissue and pick up their byproducts, which we analyze to increase our understanding of their feeding habits and assess their health. We use photography to identify individuals and drone-mounted cameras to monitor how their bodies change with the seasons and time. We deploy satellite tags, which allow us to follow their movements and learn about their encounters in places beyond our view. We adapt existing equipment; for example, instruments developed by surveyors are used to track, from the comfort of land, how whales move in the presence of boats. We collect data to help us tell the stories of their lives—who they spend time with, how they feed, and so much more.

Before humans realized that a living whale could tell us more than a dead one, we learned from the carcasses of animals killed by whalers or washed up on beaches. The history of whaling deserves a chapter of its own (see Chapter 9), but it is pertinent here to highlight the use of data gathered through this industry. Of particular interest is the illegal whaling campaign launched by the Soviets, one of the twentieth century's most notorious environmental crimes. Scientists aboard Russian whaling vessels hunting Blue Whales (*Balaenoptera musculus*) in the northern Indian Ocean kept meticulous notes on various aspects of the whales, including their length, blubber thickness, testes' weight, ovary maturation, and more. These data were kept hidden for decades because the hunts contravened international law. Subsequently, the thousands of whales killed were distilled into data points, and once revealed, the data were used to understand the hunted populations better. While whaling is not condoned, the data provided insight into the lives of whales—as well as revealing to the world the true extent of Soviet illegal whaling during the 1990s.

Fortunately, most of what we know today we have learned—and continue to learn—from live whales in the wild. This has required us to innovate: We have expanded our capacity to build tools that can withstand underwater pressures that we will never experience and have limited understanding of, and adapted everyday tools for tasks such as collecting vital samples.

Pictures to tell a story

A fundamental question in conservation, no matter what species is being studied, is, "How many are there?" For whales, the honest answer is that we don't fully know, but we can estimate using various techniques.

Photo identification is a low-cost method of estimating population size. It relies on photographs of specific parts of a whale's body—often the dorsal fin and flank and/or tail fluke—and an ability to seek out the tiny and sometimes not-so-tiny permanent markings, such as pigmentation patterns carried from birth, and the nicks, cuts, and scars the whales accumulate throughout their lives; these can be matched to other photographs to identify the same individual at different stages in its life. Importantly, these identifiers must be permanent to be usable in the long term. Much like our fingerprints, the markings on whales are individual-specific and therefore make them individually identifiable. While the process is slow and depends on researchers returning to sea year after year to carefully and meticulously photograph every individual that passes by, and subsequently comparing those photographs with the growing catalogs stored locally, regionally, and sometimes globally, it is a robust and cost-effective method that provides an opportunity for whale-watchers and enthusiasts to contribute to the endeavor, and thereby to participate in science. These photographs tell stories. Photographing a single whale in the same place over a season might indicate that the individual benefits from that area—perhaps it offers good

IDENTIFYING FEATURES
*A whale's markings are individual-specific, allowing scientists to track the
animal over time and reveal information about its health and migratory habits.*

feeding opportunities. Photographing several individuals year after year in the same area might highlight the need to protect that habitat because of what it provides the population in the long term, such as a safe nursery area for bringing up calves or a healthy feeding ground. Photographing an individual across ocean basins tells us about its movements and migrations. From seeing an animal consistently over ten years from birth, we might know that it is ten years old, while seeing it ten years in a row from adulthood allows us to assume that it is at least 15–20 years old. If an adult appears with a young calf by its side, we assume that the adult is a female, and that the pair represent a mother and a calf. By studying the same nicks and cuts on their bodies that we use to recognize them, we learn about the threats they face or the illnesses they carry.

This simple technique can reveal fascinating stories about the lives of these giants. In 2020, Riptide, an Orca (*Orcinus orca*) regularly spotted off Iceland, made a dash for Beirut, Lebanon, where it was photographed. As well as being a first record of the species off Beirut, this resulted in the documenting of what is potentially the longest Orca migration in the world—over 5,000 miles (8,000km).

* * *

This is where Whalentine comes in. Whalentine is the oldest known Blue Whale in the northern Indian Ocean, so named for the heart-shaped scar on the bottom right side of its tail fluke. While I was documenting it on a foray off the east coast of Sri Lanka in 2011, my gut sense was that I had seen it before. Following up on my instinct led me to the only Sri Lankan Blue Whale photo ID research paper ever written prior to the launch of my own research. The paper contained a handful of photographs of whale flukes, one of which was of the same individual. The heart-shaped mark was a dead giveaway, but there were other features, such as a dip on the top of the fluke and some white scars in the middle, that clinched it for me. That said, by 2011 the whale did have a few more scars, but we all know that these are a gift that comes with old age. It was exciting to think that this at least and likely over 27-year-old was the oldest known Blue Whale in our waters. Moreover, I spotted it a mere 6 miles (10 km) from where it was initially seen 27 years before. While I cannot know its whereabouts or activities during the intervening years, we can assume that the individual favored this particular space, and its return indicated a level of site fidelity.

Tracking whales from the air

It is also possible to estimate population sizes from the air. All you need is two willing observers to document sightings of whales from a fixed-wing aircraft. To do this, the observers peer out of a bubble window, which lets them count and record everything they see below them. To ensure they don't only swoop over areas with the biggest gatherings or most interesting species, the scientists commit to predesigned transects: travel paths designed to ensure good, representative coverage over an area of interest. Aerial surveys have the distinct advantage of covering vast areas quickly. Well-designed transects take into account how long a whale takes to travel from one area to another to ensure no whales are counted more than once. This is of utmost importance for accurately estimating population size. By repeating the same transects year after year, scientists can unravel whether the populations might be increasing, decreasing, or stabilizing, and whether or not they return to familiar areas annually or redistribute themselves as environmental conditions change.

Given that not everyone can find a fixed-wing aircraft or the funds to hire one, these same methods can be adapted for use off a boat—with two observers standing up front and scanning the horizon across 180 degrees in front of them. Again, the transect's predetermined travel path keeps them on the straight and narrow. Understandably, coverage is more limited, given the speed of a vessel relative to an aircraft. Still, this method has been used for assessing populations of a range of cetaceans worldwide.

SAFETY IN NUMBERS
Traveling in pods provides opportunities for toothed whales, like sperm whales, to socialize, and offers protection against predators.

Tracking whales from space

There is also growing potential for using satellites to detect and count live whales and identify stranded ones, particularly in remote and hard-to-reach places—which is to say a large part of our planet. Whales-from-space research is still in its infancy and has a few things to iron out, including the costs associated with accessing satellite imagery, the lack of satellites, and the difficulty of finding the largest animals on the planet in a highly pixelated and immense snapshot of the deep-blue ocean. However, the potential of this method and its applications is huge, and scientists see it as a worthy investment, particularly if artificial intelligence (AI) can be trained to scour through the images and identify whales reliably. It was using satellite imagery that researchers recently identified a North Atlantic Right Whale known as Ruffian from space—a first for this species. He was recognized based on his pattern of callosities and a distinctive entanglement scar on his back.

While the numbers are important and form the basis of most conservation conversations, other mysteries need to be unraveled regarding these elusive species. Much of what we know about their fine-scale movements only became possible with the invention of the satellite tag, a beacon attached to the whale's body, typically on its dorsal flank. The dorsal flank is ideal because as a whale rises to the surface to breathe, this is the first part of the body to be exposed, allowing the tag to reliably ping its position every time the whale surfaces. Researchers sitting at their desks can then follow the journey of their study species remotely and in real time. Combining this with information about ocean phenomena such as currents, fronts, and circulation patterns can build a story about the journey undertaken. To extrapolate the movements for an entire population, tags must be deployed on a minimum number of individuals—certainly more than one—and fingers are crossed that they stay on for a sufficient duration to elucidate the very private lives of the whales as they venture beyond the confines of our study areas. Data from satellite tags have helped scientists build a picture of whale movements within high-threat areas like shipping lanes and to recognize areas important to a particular population—enabling us to target our conservation efforts effectively.

Tracking whales underwater

Tags not only tell us where a species travels in horizontal space; sometimes they tell us about movements in vertical space. Suction cup tags are short-term tags with no satellite capability, which are deployed on a whale to gain an understanding of its underwater movement patterns. These tags have a timed release or burn wire that releases the tag from the whale's body after a predetermined amount of time, after which it floats to the surface. Once at the surface, this tag must be located, often using VHF, and collected so that the data can be downloaded. Data can relate to how deep the whale went and for how long, how fast it moved over specific segments, whether it turned left or right, the temperature zones it passed through on its journey, and where exactly it lunged for a mouthful of its favorite prey. The data are pieced together to get a sense of a "day in the life" of the tagged whale. These tags have provided fascinating insights, from how deep the deepest diving whale is known to go—a tagged Cuvier's Beaked Whale (*Ziphius cavirostris*) dove to 9,816 ft (2,992 m) over 3 hours and 42 minutes in a single breath!—to the gentle pirouetting that Blue Whales do when they find a patch of food.

WHALE OBSERVATION
Satellite tags enable scientists to observe whales' migratory habits as well as identify parts of the ocean where they may be vulnerable to many anthropogenic threats.

REVEALING THE SECRETS OF BODY PARTS AND BYPRODUCTS

Historically, if boats approached whales, it was bad news. Today, a boat approaching may be carrying scientists seeking to help protect the whales by undertaking research.

Secrets of blubber

Such research may involve attaching a tag or collection of a biopsy sample. For the latter, scientists use specially designed crossbows or pneumatic rifles to shoot small darts at the dorsal flank, right behind the dorsal fin of a whale. The hollow dart then bounces off the whale, holding a small plug of skin and blubber the size of a pencil eraser; these float on the surface until picked up for analysis. This tiny piece of blubber can reveal much about the life of the whale it was collected from. It can be used to identify the species and holds a wealth of genetic information that tells us about the population structure, including the individual's sex and relatedness to others. Hormones in the blubber tell us about the whale's sexual maturity, reproductive cycles, stress levels, and whether or not an animal is pregnant. We can also learn about the diet of the whales and even whether they have ingested chemicals, including persistent organic pollutants (POPs). While biopsies are a good way to collect blubber samples, blubber can also be reliably collected during necropsies and used for hormone analysis postmortem. Importantly, scientists are cautious when taking biopsy samples and do not approach when very young calves are present or if an animal looks visibly distressed.

Dandruff and feces

Whales often dive to the depths to feed, and when they emerge at the surface for a breath of air, they sometimes simultaneously leave behind gifts for the keen observer. Sloughed skin and feces might seem like things to overlook and ignore, but whale dandruff is far more important than that of humans and can

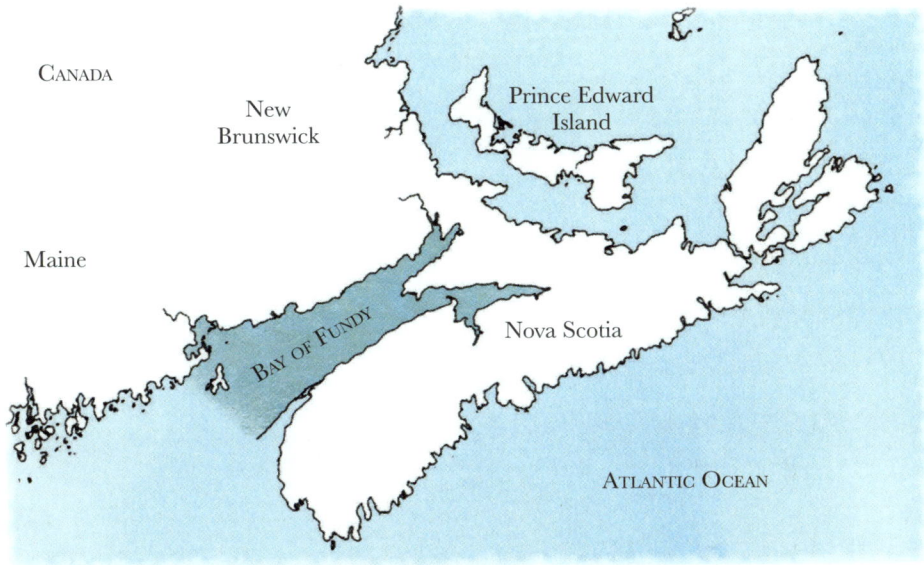

THE BAY OF FUNDY
*Whales' stress levels correlate with noise levels in the ocean, as revealed
through North Atlantic Right Whale feces collected in the Bay of Fundy.*

be used to determine the sex of individuals; whale feces, or poop, reveals secrets
about the elusive lives of these beasts. Fundamentally, feces is digested prey
matter. By extracting the DNA of the prey that has been consumed and excreted, it is possible to identify what makes up the diet of these whales. It has limitations in that you cannot quantify what has been consumed, but it can provide a sense of the general diet. While Blue Whales across the world are known
to feast on krill in vast quantities, in Sri Lankan waters, an analysis of their
feces and DNA metabarcoding revealed that these tropical whales predominantly feast on a type of shrimp. Given that this shrimp is more prevalent than
krill around Sri Lanka, this makes sense. But it also reminds us not to take
everything for granted in a species that, while very large and obvious at the
ocean surface, is often unseen and lurks quietly in our global oceans.

Fecal matter is also important for understanding stress in whales, particularly that linked to "invisible" threats like underwater noise. In an elegant study
conducted by scientists at the New England Aquarium, North Atlantic Right

DRONE "SNOT BOT"
Drones can be used to collect exhaled air from a whale to help in the study of stress and whale microbiomes.

Whale (*Eubalaena glacialis*) fecal samples collected before, soon after, and signifi-cantly after the 9/11 terrorist attacks were analyzed for stress hormones. Researchers made a surprising discovery. Ironically, while humans were much more on edge and stressed immediately after the attacks, whales became more relaxed, with decreased baseline levels of stress-related fecal hormone metabo-lites. This was because the shutdown of shipping in the Bay of Fundy immedi-ately post 9/11 reduced noise levels in the ocean significantly. This reduction in shipping translated into quieter oceans for whales, resulting in reduced stress levels. No sooner had shipping recommenced than their stress levels increased once again. This study encapsulates the power of feces in understanding the private lives of whales—in this case, endangered North Atlantic Right Whales. Stress can also be measured using other tools. The famed "snot bot," a modi-fied drone that can collect "snot," "blow," or exhaled air from a whale's blow-hole—with the aid of a skilled pilot and a petri dish—has opened doors to the study of stress and the analysis of DNA and microbiomes.

Stomach contents

While much messier, stomach analyses can also give us insight into a whale's diet. When a dead whale strands, experts with the right equipment spend hours or even days performing necropsies on the deteriorating carcass. In a race against time, scientists will prioritize identifying the cause of death, but once that has been done, they will use the carcass to reconstruct the life of the whale. Analysis of stomach contents is a common way to investigate the diet of almost any species. However, accessing the stomach of a whale is not quite the same as accessing the stomach of a fish, and once accessed, storing the insides is no mean feat. However, a thorough analysis of what lies within can often provide insights into whales' preferred food and even the parasites they carry.

Baleen

Baleen is another keeper of endocrine secrets. Growing from front to back, where shedding occurs over time, baleen represents a distinct stretch of the whale's life. This structure, made of keratin, much like our hair and nails, is

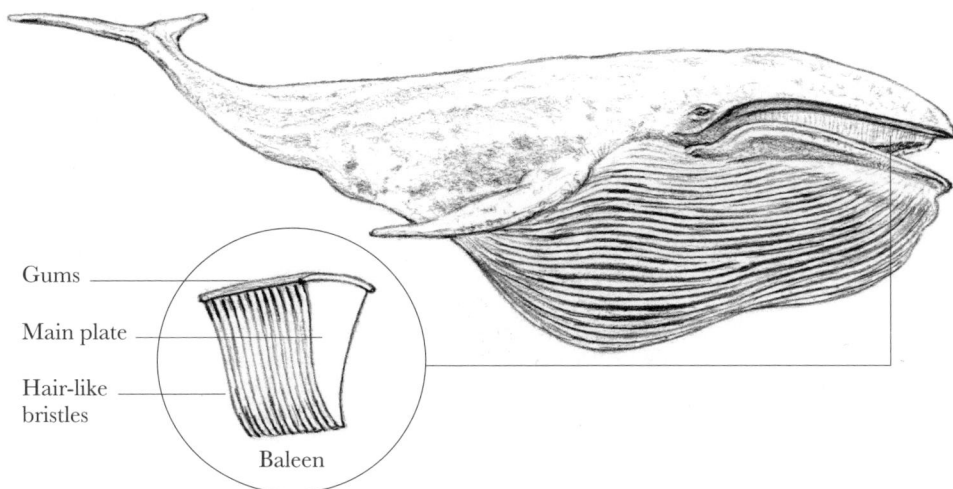

Gums
Main plate
Hair-like bristles
Baleen

BALEEN
Made from keratin, this filter-feeding system allows scientists to unlock the hormonal histories of individual whales.

more than just a filter-feeding apparatus, as it incorporates hormones as it grows. Each plate is, therefore, a multi-year record of detailed endocrine-related information waiting to be interpreted. Scientists use these plates to study testosterone patterns of male whales in order to understand more about reproductive seasonality, the breeding season, and the individual's life history.

Items left behind

Despite their stressful lives, many whale species have long lives. Blue Whales and Humpback Whales (*Megaptera novaeangliae*) are thought to live for 80–90 years, while Orcas live for 30–46 years, depending on their sex. But the clear winner for the longest lifespan is the Bowhead Whale (*Balaena mysticetus*), which is thought to live for well over a century. This discovery was made in 2007 when Indigenous hunters on Utqiaġvik (known to some as Barrow Island), Alaska, hunted (under permit) a Bowhead Whale and found a "bomb lance" inside it. This harpoon, infused with gunpowder that explodes on contact—used to hunt whales in the Arctic in the past—had lodged itself in the blubber of the whale, which had escaped only to be caught once again over a century later.

Fortunately, finding stone harpoon heads lodged in carcasses is not the only way to age whales. Aging of whales can be done using the eye lens protein racemization method. Essentially, the lens of a whale's eye contains crystalline

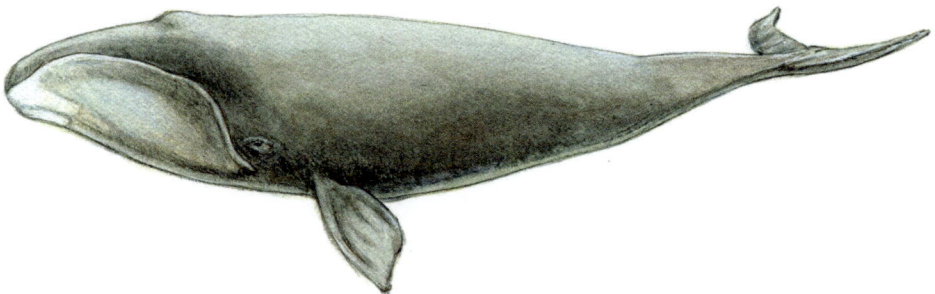

BOWHEAD WHALE
The protein in the eye lens of a whale can provide the key to unlocking its age.

proteins that are formed before or shortly after birth, and which remain the same throughout the animal's life. The proteins undergo a process known as amino acid racemization, whereby the tiny building blocks of proteins (called amino acids) gradually convert from the L-form (used by living organisms to build proteins) to the D-form (a mirror image of the L-form not used in protein building). In the whale's eye lens, the conversion of the amino acid aspartic acid happens at a slow and predictable pace, so when scientists measure how much of the L-form has turned in to the D-form, they can estimate how long the process has been happening and estimate the whale's age. This technique was used to verify the age of the Bowhead Whale that was hunted in 2007.

Whales' ear wax or ear plugs also offer an opportunity for aging, with alternate light and dark bands representing summer binges and winter migrations. Counting these bands is an alternative means of aging whales.

WHALE SONG

Finally, but no less important, is how we have learned about the sounds whales make. Whales have learned to use sound in powerful ways to communicate over vast distances. But human and whale hearing ranges do not overlap for the most part, so we cannot always detect their sounds without the assistance of hydrophones (underwater microphones). These allow us to eavesdrop and record their chatter, and then speed up those sounds to a point where we can hear even those that communicate at the lowest frequencies, like Blue Whales. In some cases, scientists drop recording equipment to the bottom of the ocean for months to capture the comings and goings of all marine mammal species in the area. Ultimately, they are faced with vast quantities of data—recordings of whale songs and ocean noise—not all of which interest them. Listening to it all and picking out the "whale-like" sounds can take a hours, days, months, or more, depending on the size of the dataset; so to speed things up, researchers sometimes extract a sample and program detectors to trawl through and identify other similar calls automatically. AI is now used to analyze even larger datasets in order to find and unravel more about the language of the whales. Work by Project CETI (Cetacean Translation Initiative) claims to have uncovered a "sperm whale phonetic alphabet," but there is much speculation about what that means. One thing is certain: We still have a way to go before we can converse with these animals.

* * *

A combination of human ingenuity and technology has allowed us to explore the lives of whales. The understanding we have gained has given us insight into parts of their lives that would otherwise go unseen. While there is beauty in not knowing everything, a basic understanding of other creatures who share our planet allows us to grow in empathy for their needs and provides us with the knowledge necessary to protect them and the habitats within which they live.

3

WHAT MAKES
A WHALE
A WHALE?

WHALE DESIGN

Good design is beautiful, efficient, and, most importantly, functional. Well-designed animals are generally more likely to survive and thrive in their environment: Camouflage helps animals avoid predators, vibrant plumage helps them find mates, thicker fur enables them to live in colder climates, and specialized feeding mechanisms enable them to exploit and thrive in different ecological niches. This is where the study of anatomy becomes important. Anatomy is essentially the parts, both internal and external, of an animal's body. Studying anatomy is particularly useful in species like whales that spend most of their lives underwater and out of view. Their anatomy provides clues that allow us to hypothesize about their lives, even the parts we do not see.

For a start, whales generally have streamlined bodies that are propelled by their tail flukes, which are attached to the body by the peduncle. We will discuss these various body parts in more detail shortly but the need for a streamlined body is particularly pertinent as whales spend the majority of their lives moving through water, a medium that is 800 times denser and 55 times more viscous than air, resulting in water having a higher resistance to flow and being more difficult to maneuver through. Despite their large size, being streamlined—and thus well-designed—means that whales can move through the ocean efficiently, expending minimal energy as they do so. This is a crucial factor, particularly for species that travel vast distances during their migrations. The reduced costs of locomotion are important as some whales, such as Humpback Whales (*Megaptera novaeangliae*), embark on migratory journeys during which they do not feed for months.

That said, not all whales are created equal. While some, like Fin Whales (*Balaenoptera physalus*), are long and slender and can reach high speeds, others, like Humpbacks and Right Whales (*Eubalaena glacialis, E. japonica, E. australis*), are rounder and slower-moving. The speeds at which they travel are likely driven by the food they choose to eat. If you have food that can zip out of the way instantly, your need for speed is higher.

Dorsal fin | Dorsal ridge

Rostrum | Two blowholes | Axillae

Caudal peduncle

Anus   Flukes

Baleen

Urogenital slit

Pectoral flippers

Ventral pleats (in rorquals only) | Umbilicus | Mammary glands

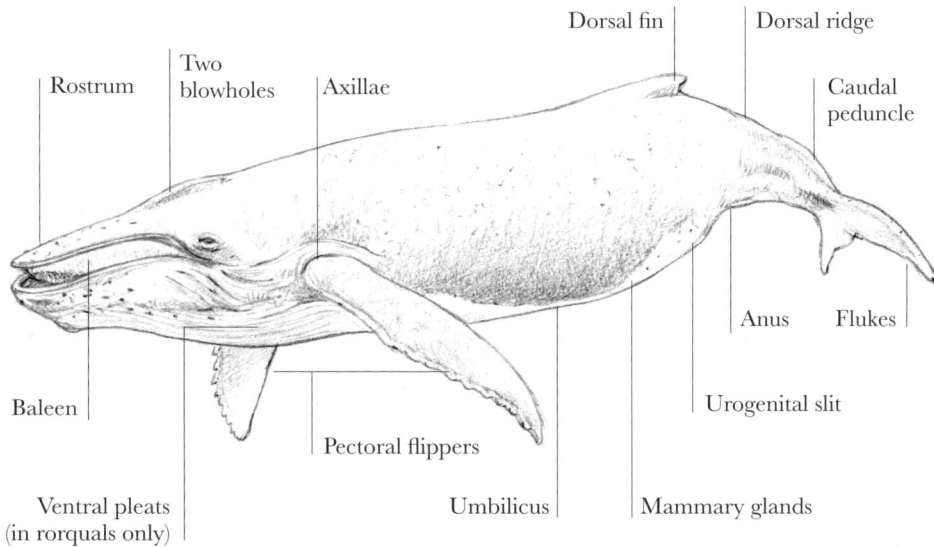

BASIC WHALE ANATOMY
All whales have flippers, flukes, and either teeth or baleen.

WHALE GIGANTISM

Baleen whales are the undisputed champions of being large. As it turns out, whale gigantism is closely tied to two things. The first is lunge feeding, a feeding technique that initially came into being 7–10 MYA and was perfected by the rorquals; it was favored by those with larger mouths (and therefore larger bodies) rather than those with smaller mouths, and lunge feeding is a defining feature of rorquals. The second was the parallel increase, about 5 MYA, of ocean upwelling, where water is rich in nutrients thanks to organisms decomposing, leading to nitrogen and phosphorous release driving increases in phytoplankton blooms. This resulted in an increase in productivity across the board—including an increase in prey availability. The combination of these two phenomena—a new and appropriate feeding strategy and the availability of ample prey—led to the rather recent evolution of Earth's largest animals.

Within this overall increase in rorqual size, one species, the Blue Whale (*Balaenoptera musculus*), stands out as the largest by far. While Blue Whales are only about 20 ft (6 m) longer than their cousins the Fin Whales, they weigh about twice as much (with females being about 5 percent larger than males, perhaps due to increased blubber content that provides energy necessary to nurture their calves). In a world filled with competitors, Blue Whales are picky eaters and became fiercely specialized at hunting and feeding on one thing and one thing alone: krill. Krill are a swarming species of marine crustacean that are superabundant but patchy, found in upwelling areas and polar seas. Blue Whales' dependence on this specific prey has resulted in a large-bodied animal with the ability to travel efficiently through water and maintain large energy reserves for times when their favorite food is less abundant. Their need to travel vast distances between prey patches and access food prioritized a need for speed, trumping a need for extreme maneuverability, resulting in them growing bigger and developing a larger mouth that can take in more krill with each bite (lunge). Maintaining this size requires more food, which in turn requires a larger body and mouth to access, and so on, leading to Blue Whales becoming the largest whales on Earth. Weaned Minke Whales (*Balaenoptera acutorostrata, B. bonaerensis*), at a mere 15 ft (4.5 m) in length, are the absolute minimum size that a rorqual can be while still eating enough food to survive.

A MINKE WHALE
Minke Whales are small and elusive. They can be difficult to track, even for researchers.

BLUE WHALES
These giants of the ocean evolved from ancestors such as the extinct Maiabalaena nesbittae.

To exemplify just how large Blue Whales are, let me tell you a quick story. I was once out on a boat in Monterey Bay, California, watching a large pod of dolphins pass by. Soon, a number of Humpback Whales appeared and began to put on an incredible display of lunge feeding. If you have never seen a whale lunge feed, I would recommend it as one of the most awe-inspiring sights ever. The tourists onboard were awed by the whales' size, particularly in relation to the dolphins that had just whizzed by. After a while, the Humpbacks dived and vanished from view. A few moments of quiet and then "Whoosh!!"—the powerful blow of what could only be a Blue Whale grabbed the attention of everyone on board. People could not believe it as I told them it was a Blue Whale. It was my first Pacific blue sighting and I was as ecstatic as everyone else. Moments later, a Humpback Whale popped back up to the surface, in front of the Blue Whale. Someone exclaimed "Oh! The dolphins are back!" The immense size of the Blue Whale dwarfed the Humpback sufficiently to make people believe it was just a dolphin!

Returning to the topic of feeding, I should point out that in Sri Lankan waters, Pygmy Blue Whales (*Balaenoptera musculus indica*)—the Blue Whale subspecies that lives in the northern Indian Ocean—do not specialize in eating krill but sergestid

53

shrimp. This is simply because the sergestid shrimp is the dominant swarming species in these waters. While we know little about their feeding behaviors in this part of the world, research indicates that these whales are feeding deeper in the water column than any other Blue Whale population, and this could be because sergestid shrimp are found deeper than krill. This serves to remind us that no two whales are the same, and we cannot take it for granted that whales of the same species living in different ocean basins will act the same way.

It is clear that being big has its advantages, including being able to avoid predation by being too quick to hunt down or simply too large to attack, traveling effortlessly and with energetic efficiency between prey patches, using less energy to keep warm, building fat stores quickly, and being able to go long periods without feeding. But there are disadvantages to weighing so much. While the issue of a heavier skeleton is circumvented through having mostly light and spongy bones, this species is still bulky (a Blue Whale's heart weighs about 400 lb, or 180 kg, and is around 5 ft tall). In the ocean there is plenty of space and food, and the weight of the whale's body is supported by seawater, unlike on land, where animals have to support their own weight against the force of gravity, making it impossible to achieve such enormity. Blue Whales are, in fact, neutrally buoyant: Their density matches their surroundings, so they float.

LOCOMOTION AND MANEUVERABILITY

Flukes and flippers

The power whales need to achieve the speeds they do comes from their tails, or flukes. This fluke structure is flexible and strong, extends beyond the bony vertebral column, and provides a clue to their evolutionary past (See Chapter 1). Unlike fish, whose tails move from side to side, whales undulate in an upward–

downward motion with the help of longitudinal muscles in the back and caudal peduncle (where the flukes meet the body). This is because cetaceans have horizontal tail flukes, which evolved from their land-dwelling, four-legged ancestors, whose backbones bent up and down to extend their spine and stride while running. In whales, the aspect ratio of flukes (the ratio of fluke width to height), can indicate whether they are fast or slow movers. Similar height-to-width proportions of their flippers can indicate their maneuverability. Together, they tell us a bit about the whale's life and feeding behaviors.

Blue Whales are designed for speed, with highly streamlined bodies and small, high aspect ratio flippers and flukes, which increases their propulsive force. While this does have downsides in that it prevents quick starts and reduces maneuverability, given that the whales' preferred prey is nonevasive, these two characteristics are not worth investing in. Instead, the ability to cruise efficiently from one patch of food to the next in the open ocean is a high priority. Right Whales, on the other hand, are rotund, less streamlined, and have flukes with a large surface area and high aspect ratio. These features make them efficient cruisers too, but their preference is for slow movement. This fits well with their feeding requirements, as they are designed optimally for continuous filter feeding as they push through the water column, open mouthed, to feed on zooplankton. This constant open-mouth method of skim feeding, coupled with their large heads, introduces a lot of drag, which a large propulsive tail can overcome.

What some whales lose in speed, they gain in maneuverability. Humpback Whales are a fantastic case in point. With their large, high aspect ratio flippers —notably the largest appendages of any animal on Earth, growing to 20 ft (6 m)—and large, low aspect ratio tail, they can accelerate rapidly and even perform tight 180-degree rolls. This works perfectly for a species that indulges in prey that tend to be evasive, and which therefore depends on techniques like bubble-net feeding. Gray Whales (*Eschrichtius robustus*) are also built to maneuver themselves at odd angles. They use their rostrum to dig for benthic prey, which means food found at the bottom of the ocean, such as amphipods, which they then filter out with their baleen. When digging, they most often roll at an angle greater than 45 degrees, a behavior confirmed by unequal baleen wear in this species.

While both flukes and flippers are designed to assist efficient locomotion and support the feeding needs of the various whale species, they are inherently different in that the fluke is made entirely of a dense, fibrous type of connective tissue while the flipper contains the same bones that we humans have in our hands. This is a reminder that whales' ancestors were land-dwelling animals with paws—just like ours. Paws were inherently unhelpful for swimming, so they evolved into paddles.

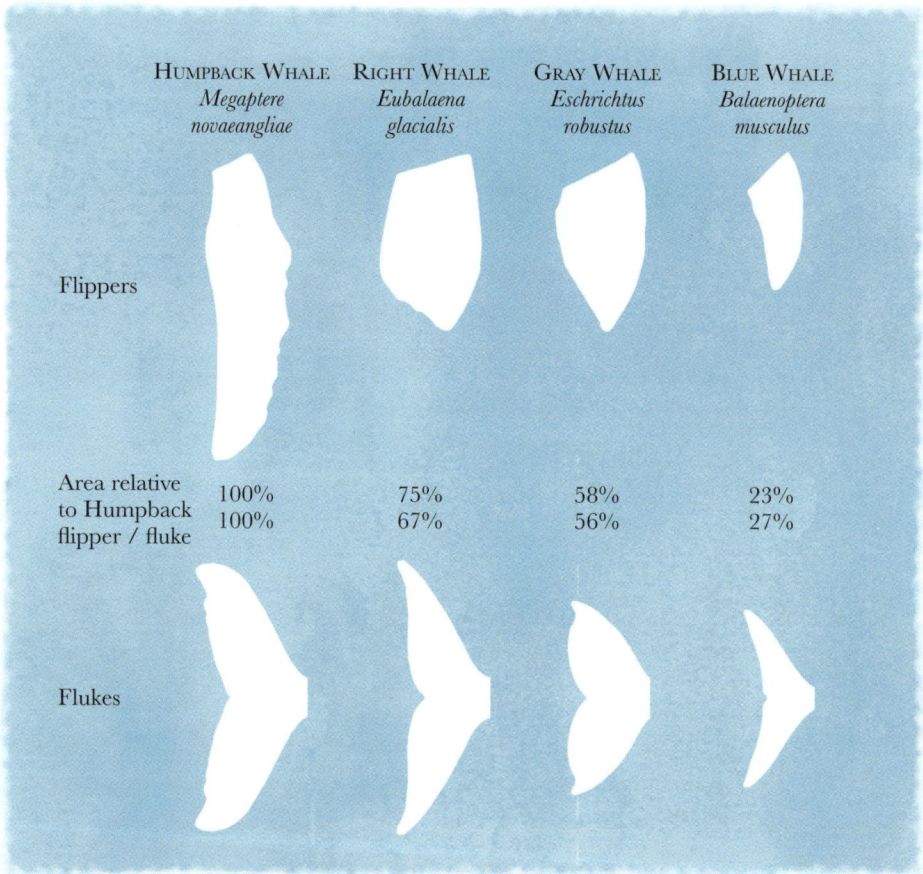

	HUMPBACK WHALE *Megaptere novaeangliae*	RIGHT WHALE *Eubalaena glacialis*	GRAY WHALE *Eschrichtus robustus*	BLUE WHALE *Balaenoptera musculus*
Flippers				
Area relative to Humpback flipper / fluke	100% 100%	75% 67%	58% 56%	23% 27%
Flukes				

FLUKES AND FLIPPERS
The areas of fins and tail flukes vary enormously between species,
with Humpbacks having by far the largest.

Dorsal fin

The fin on the back of a whale, known as the dorsal fin, is said to act like a keel and assist with stability while swimming. Whales with bigger dorsal fins are thought to attain higher speeds but possess reduced maneuverability. North Atlantic Right Whales (*E. glacialis*)—named as the "right" whales to kill partly because of their ambling pace—do not possess a dorsal fin, while Orcas (*Orcinus orca*) are the second-fastest marine mammal in our oceans and have incredibly tall dorsal fins—male Orca dorsal fins can reach as high as 6 ft (1.8 m)! That said, in species like Blue and Sperm Whales (*Physeter macrocephalus*), the dorsal fin is so small relative to their body size that it likely does not serve any purpose.

FEEDING: TEETH, BALEEN, AND VENTRAL PLEATS

While we have already divided whales into their respective groups based on their feeding structures (Chapter 1), it is pertinent to revisit these features here briefly. Teeth are typically found in species that need to capture fast-moving prey. They vary in number between species, from a few to over 200. Sperm Whales have 36–50 banana-shaped teeth in their lower jaw, which fit into sockets in their upper jaw, where they do not have any teeth. Spinner Dolphins (*Stenella longirostris*), on the other hand, have more teeth than any other dolphin species, with 45–65 teeth on each side of the upper and lower jaws.

Baleen, a keratinized comb-like structure built into the roof of the mouth of many great whales, is essentially a giant strainer used to access food. Baleen is flexible and tough and is found in the mouths of some of the largest species because it allows them to capture a huge number of small creatures all at once.

The color and length of baleen differ between species, with Blue Whales having short, wide, black baleen and Fin Whales having black baleen on the left jaw and white on the right jaw.

Given the sheer amount of food these whales require to fulfill their energetic requirements, they need large heads to accommodate it all. To deal with this and the issues of drag that would come into play if their heads were bulbous and large, they have developed ventral pleats. Ventral pleats, the stripes extending from under the whale's chin to its belly button, are not just for aesthetics but are functional. When the whale finds a patch of food, its lower jaw opens to 90 degrees and takes in a mouthful of water and prey.

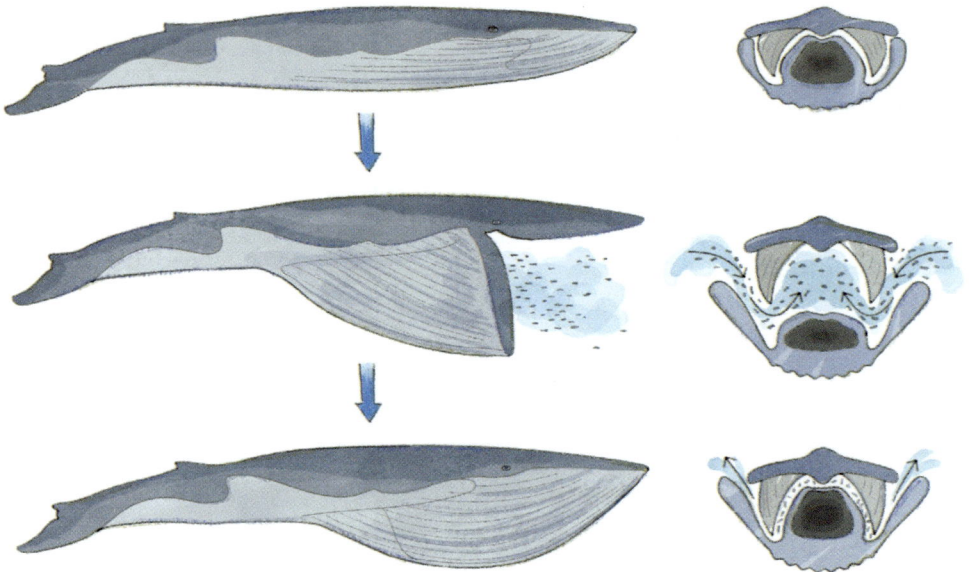

BALEEN WHALE VENTRAL PLEATS
Ventral pleats in baleen whales are accordion-like structures under their chin that they can use to expand their gulp to engulf a mouthful of prey.

Their accordion-like ventral pleats then expand according to the volume of engulfed water—the pouch can expand so much that it exceeds the volume of the whale itself. But this is all temporary, with the whale using its tongue to expel the water through its baleen, and any prey stuck in the baleen is then swallowed. The advantage of these ventral pleats is obvious—while they enable the whales to make the most of large patches of food, they are easily contracted at other times, enabling the whale to remain streamlined as it moves through the ocean.

Interestingly, the length and number of ventral pleats are important features in distinguishing different species of baleen whales. In some, like Blue Whales and Humpbacks, they end at the belly button, while in Sei (*Balaenoptera borealis*) and Minke Whales, they do not extend so far. Bryde's Whales (*Balaenoptera edeni*) have fewer ventral pleats (42–54) than Blue Whales (90–95). While it is rare to see a whale belly up, this little-known fact is beneficial when investigating a stranded specimen.

While most baleen whales depend on the combination of baleen and ventral pleats to feed, some, like the Right Whales, do not have any pleats, despite possessing baleen. This is because, unlike many of the whales that lunge at their prey swarms, Right Whales swim with their mouths open at all times and filter feed continuously, negating the need for increased space. Bowhead Whales (*Balaena mysticetus*), with their record-breaking 13-ft-long (4-m) baleen plates, have the largest mouth in relation to their body length. They, too, are continuous ram feeders who swim slowly through prey concentrations for long periods with their jaws wide open. The central gap between the two baleen plates in the front allows prey-laden water to flow continuously through their mouths, negating the need for ventral plates.

While most toothed whales have skipped the need for ventral pleats because they catch what they want and chow it down, beaked whales like Cuvier's Beaked Whales (*Ziphius cavirostris*) bend the rule by having a pair of ventral throat grooves that help to create a vacuum within their mouths, allowing them to suck in their targeted prey very efficiently.

BREATHING: BLOWHOLES AND LUNGS

As mammals, whales must breathe air and thus come up to the surface to do so. Their nostrils, or blowholes, are located at the top of the head as that is the first part of their body to reach the surface when they emerge after a big dive. This means they do not have to bring their whole head out of the water to take a breath, making the process faster and also energetically more efficient.

While it may seem that these blowholes are designed to keep seawater out, recent work suggests the opposite. Whales, including Humpback Whales, have been documented routinely inhaling seawater, which likely means that water enters their upper respiratory tract. This is largely unproblematic except when whales swim through toxic pollutants, such as oil.

BLOWHOLES
A whale's blowholes, the equivalent of our nostrils, are under voluntary control.

A whale's blowholes are directly connected to its lungs. Every time they breathe, Blue Whales purportedly exchange 80–90 percent of the oxygen in their lungs, compared with the 10–15 percent in humans. This is despite the fact that their lungs constitute 3 percent of their body cavity while human lungs make up 7 percent of ours. This efficiency is vital, given that whales have limited time at the surface and must restock on sufficient air for the long dives ahead.

RESTING

Contrary to how humans breathe, the blowhole in cetaceans is under voluntary control, and they must be "awake" to breathe. This means that, unlike humans, they must think about each breath they take, 24 hours a day. Complete shutdown of the system during sleep is therefore dangerous, and whales have developed a means of shutting down just half their brain at a time as they float at the surface resting. As they rest, they switch which hemisphere of the brain is awake. This unihemispheric sleep enables swimming, voluntary breathing, predator avoidance, and social contact. During unihemispheric sleep, the eye opposite to the waking hemisphere is fully or partially open, while the eye opposite to the sleeping hemisphere is fully or partially closed. When a whale transitions from being awake to unihemispheric sleep, the temperature in the sleeping hemisphere decreases while the temperature in the waking hemisphere remains unchanged. After a period of rest, awakening is accompanied by a gradual increase in temperature in the sleeping hemisphere.

Little is known about sleeping in wild cetaceans; however, electrophysiological studies on captive species have revealed how long and how often some species engage in unihemispheric sleeping. Bottlenose Dolphins (*Tursiops* sp.) sleep for an average of 42 minutes 2–12 times per day, Beluga Whales (*Delphinapterus leucas*) sleep for about 44 minutes, and Amazon River Dolphins (*Inia geoffrensis*) and Harbor Porpoises (*Phocoena phocoena*) sleep for longer than two hours at a

WHALES SLEEPING
Sperm Whales doze for bouts of 10–15 minutes in an upright position—head up, tail down.

time. However, while REM (rapid eye movement) sleep has been recorded in terrestrial mammals, it appears to be absent in marine mammals, which might be related to their unihemispheric pattern of sleeping.

Typically, wild whales sleep near the surface, a behavior called *logging*, because they resemble logs. Rather unusually, however, Sperm Whales have been documented sleeping vertically with their heads up and tails down. They initiate this vertical sleep by swimming down to depths of one to two times their body length, where they rotate to a head-up posture and passively drift to the surface over time. Researchers have found that Sperm Whales spend a portion of their day sleeping vertically for 10–15 minutes at a time. Hawaiian Spinner Dolphins and Dusky Dolphins (*Lagenorhynchus obscurus*) are known to rest in shallow lagoons but swim slowly in tight formations as they do so, with limited echolocation activity. Like many others, Beluga Whales lie at the surface or swim slowly in tight groups along coastlines. This continuous motion during sleep is important as swimming is life-sustaining for whales—another advantage of unihemispheric sleep.

REPRODUCING

Genitals and pelvic bones

Unlike their terrestrial counterparts, male whales do not have genitals that hang outside their body, as anything dangling outside their fusiform shape would introduce an element of drag. The penis is therefore contained inside a genital slit on the underside of the whale, emerging only when necessary. Because the penis is not visible, it can be tricky to identify gender. However, the location of this genital slit is one way to differentiate between a male and a female. In males, the genital slit is located closer to the whale's belly. Females, on the other hand, have a genital slit closer to their tail flukes, which is followed by a grapefruit-sized lump known as a hemispherical lobe.

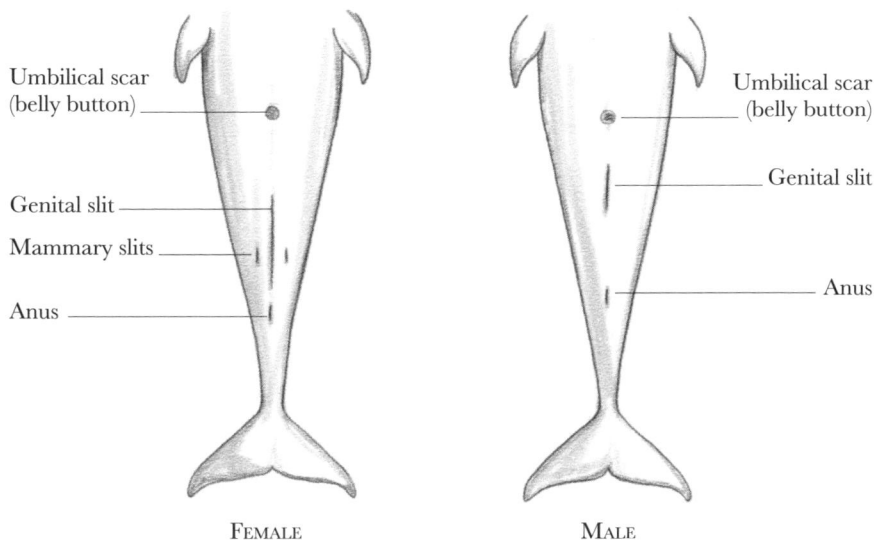

Umbilical scar (belly button)

Genital slit

Mammary slits

Anus

Umbilical scar (belly button)

Genital slit

Anus

FEMALE

MALE

GENITAL AND MAMMARY SLITS
Whale anatomy is adapted perfectly to life on the go in the ocean.

As it turns out, the pelvic bones we used to believe were vestigial in whales are in fact important in reproduction. For a long time, we assumed these bones were redundant (and that evolution would wave its magic wand and do away with them in time). However, it has turned out that the muscles that control a whale's penis attach directly to the pelvic bones, allowing for the well-known dexterity of the whale's penis.

Mammary slits

As marine mammals, whale calves depend on their mother's milk, but outwardly dangling breasts or nipples would once again introduce drag to a streamlined animal. Therefore, female whales tuck their nipples inside the two mammary slits on either side of their genital slit.

NAVIGATING THEIR WORLD

Sound

Early in development, the fetuses of all whales have similar ear structures to fetal land mammals. However, as they develop in the womb, the ears of each species begin to develop differently, indicating that they may have different ways of hearing. The acoustic funnel, a structure found in both toothed and baleen whales, is positioned differently in the two groups, so likely evolved in early whales before the two groups split 34 MYA.

Toothed whales depend on sound to find their food, but, as we know, they don't have external ears like dogs, donkeys, or ourselves. Instead, they have a fat pad embedded in the lower jaw that traps sound, which then travels to the middle ear and onward to the cochlea. Despite them having similar fat pads close to their lower jaws, baleen whale hearing remains unresolved. However, scientists describe their ears as being "as big as a human head and as dense as a bowling bowl."

Sight

The cetacean eye has had to adapt to the varying environmental challenges associated with living in an aquatic environment, which include the mechanical, chemical, osmotic, and optical conditions of living in water. Most mammals have dichromatic vision—they cannot discriminate along the red–green color axis. Overall, mammal vision is not highly developed, because our ancestors were more interested in seeing in the dark than in the light. As a result, whales have limited color vision.

In fact, whales have monochromatic vision and see the world in shades of gray. Through their eyes, the ocean is not blue but likely black. Unlike other mammals, whales appear to have lost their short-wave-sensitive cones (S-cones), which have species-dependent maximal sensitivity in the red–green and blue parts of the color spectrum.

* * *

Research suggests that this loss occurred early in the evolution of marine mammals and that the ancestors of whales probably lost their blue color vision shortly after they returned to sea.

Beyond being unable to see in color, whales also do not appear to have binocular vision, given that they have an eye on either side of their head. How they process visual information and integrate what they see (or don't see) with each eye is still a subject of speculation.

Smell

Not much is known about whales' ability to smell. But the lack of nerves required for smelling in toothed whales led people to believe that baleen whales, with whom they share a common ancestor, would also have a lousy sense of smell. However, the well-developed olfactory system in a dissected Bowhead Whale brain was perhaps the first indication that we may have underestimated the use of this sense in this species group. Bowheads may use smell to sniff the air in search of krill. Experiments with Humpback Whales at sea off Iceland have indicated that the scent of their favorite dinner might result in surface behaviors indicative of sensory exploration, such as diving under the scent and putting the brakes on. It has been suggested that those species that feed closer to the bottom of the food chain likely rely more on smell than those that feed higher up. It also turns out that the closer a baleen whale's typical prey item is to the bottom of the food chain, the wider the distance is between the two blowholes of the whale relative to its body width, suggesting that baleen whales smell in stereo. Stereo-olfaction is the ability to perceive odors or smells with both nostrils independently of one another, sending different signals to the brain that are then used to identify the direction of an odor. This ability helps them to sniff out dimethyl sulfide (DMS), a gas released by phytoplankton when it is being preyed on by zooplankton such as those that whales enjoy feeding on—ultimately leading the whales to a good meal. This hypothesis still needs testing, but it is clear that prey-derived chemical cues are important to baleen whales when hunting for prey in the vast ocean.

THERMOREGULATION

You may wonder how these warm-blooded animals stay warm while living in cold polar waters. While they have a steady core body temperature, heat loss is a continuous issue, regardless of temperature, as water conducts heat away from the body 25 times faster than air. To reduce heat loss, whales have three main adaptations that are important to explore when understanding the anatomy of this species.

The first is their surface area to volume ratio. In short, smaller mammals like shrews have greater surface area to volume ratios than larger animals like elephants, or indeed whales. This lower volume to surface area ratio means that heat loss is slower, because a smaller percentage of the total body volume is exposed to the surface—an advantage of being huge in the ocean.

The second adaptation for keeping warm is their layer of blubber. Blubber thickness can vary in whales, with Bowhead Whales having the thickest of all, and can vary with the time of year; for example, Humpback Whales have blubber layers that are around 6 in (15 cm) thick, which can increase to 20 in by the end of the feeding season. Blubber is an efficient way to keep warm, even at depths where compression occurs, as it smoothes out the whale's shape, reducing hydrodynamic drag and acting as an energy store.

Reduced surface area to volume ratios and thick blubber are great evolutionary adaptations for living in water; however, what happens when whales swim fast or are in warmer water than they are used to? How do they dump the excess heat that blubber prevents them losing? The answer is that they have certain sneaky spots that lack blubber and are not well insulated,

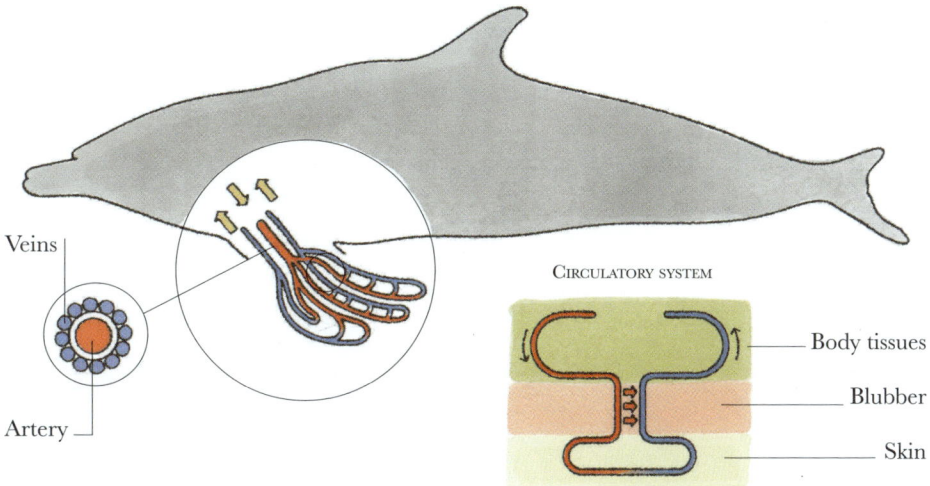

Veins

Artery

CIRCULATORY SYSTEM

Body tissues

Blubber

Skin

COUNTER-CURRENT HEAT EXCHANGE

This ingenious system means warm-blooded whales can easily manage their core body temperatures at all times. The magnified area on the left shows blood vessels arranged closely together, specifically arteries (red) and veins (blue) running in opposite directions. This arrangement allows warm arterial blood from the body core to transfer heat to the cooler venous blood returning from the extremities. The schematic on the right shows heat moving from the red vessel to the blue one as blood flows in opposite directions. This counter-current flow conserves body heat by preventing it from being lost to the environment at the surface of the skin.

termed *thermal windows*, such as their flippers, dorsal fins, and flukes. Relative to the blubber, these areas are thin and highly vascularized. Having arteries and veins that run close to each other means that blood of different temperatures flowing in different directions transfers heat across the membranes in an efficient system called the *counter-current heat exchanger*. Warm blood leaving the heart passes heat to the cooler returning blood from the extremities—like the fluke—conserving heat and minimizing loss to the surrounding cold water.

Since species like Bowhead Whales spend long periods at the surface with their mouths open when feeding, they have an organ called the *corpus cavernosum maxillaris*, a bulbous ridge of highly vascularized tissue in the soft palette of their mouth. This organ acts as a counter-current heat exchange system and prevents the excessive loss of heat from their bodies, perhaps even protecting the brain from hypothermia.

4

STARTING FROM THE VERY BEGINNING

CONCEPTION, GESTATION, AND PREGNANCY

Whale reproduction is a costly exercise. The energy it requires diverts from other crucial activities like growth, immune function, and self-maintenance, and can have huge impacts on a female whale's overall health and survival.

Both toothed and baleen whales invest heavily in the gestation and growth of their offspring. This means that environmental shifts and the varied availability of prey in the ocean require whales to weigh up the commitment of rearing a calf with that of their own survival. In long-lived animals such as whales, this trade-off, combined with their dedicated parental investment in offspring, can even result in a miscarriage or abandonment of a calf. Blue Whale (*Balaenoptera musculus*) and Southern Right Whale (*Eubalaena australis*) females follow this reproductive strategy whereby they prioritize their own body condition and reserves over carrying a pregnancy to term or raising a calf in poor conditions. If the female is weakened due to a lack of food or environmental stress, she may miscarry or abandon a calf to ensure she can recover and increase her chances of successfully reproducing in the next season. This means that she maintains shorter calving intervals and ensures she has the necessary fat stores and energy to provide her next born with sufficient milk for survival. While this strategy results in occasional losses, elephants and primates also use it to maximize reproductive success over time.

Reproductive rates

In many species of baleen whales, their reproductive cycle is closely tied to their migratory cycle, which requires them to undertake annual long-range migrations between feeding and calving grounds. The reproductive cycle, which is a minimum of two years, starts with mating, followed by calving in the wintering grounds, and ends with the weaning of calves before they arrive at the feeding grounds during their first summer.

Southern Right Whale and North Atlantic Right Whale (*Eubalaena glacialis*) females, however, have longer reproductive cycles due to their slower maturation and extended parental care. Each cycle comprises one year each of gestation, lactation, and a three- to ten-year calving interval during which they rest to recover energy stores before they start it all over again. The lengthening of the calving interval from an average of three years to ten years is a result of the increasing environmental stress this species is under.

In general, toothed whales have slower reproductive rates than baleen whales, with Sperm Whale (*Physeter macrocephalus*) mothers having the slowest reproductive rates among all cetaceans. Such is the case in species that have strong social structures who invest heavily in parental care. In Sperm Whales, individuals have a 14–16-month gestation period and produce a single calf of about 13 ft (4 m) every 4–6 years, indicating a significant investment in care that leads to a longer calving interval. Sperm Whale females are also not constrained by a migratory cycle, because they live in their social units at tropical latitudes throughout their lives. The long-term care provided to offspring does not just slow down reproductive rates but, given the fewer mating opportunities, becomes a significant incentive for choosing a high-quality male with which to mate.

Stages of gestation

Within the first few months, the fetus becomes increasingly recognizable as a whale. At about seven to eight months, a Humpback (*Megaptera novaeangliae*) fetus takes on the unmistakable characteristics of the adult, with the development of long, knobbly flippers. (I once visited the last whaling station in Australia, located in Albany, Western Australia, and came face to face with a Sperm Whale fetus in a jar that had been extracted from the womb of its mother who had been hunted. I guess I was not expecting it, but the fetus was an absolute bonsai version of a full-grown sperm whale, despite being only about 2 ft in length (Sperm Whales are typically born at nearly 15 ft). Interestingly, baleen whales in utero actually do have teeth. These "baby" teeth are unique to the early fetal stage, after which they are reabsorbed and replaced by baleen. The presence of teeth, even for this fleeting time, is a reminder of the shared ancestry of baleen and toothed whales.

For a baleen whale mother in the early stages of gestation (the first and second trimester), she is still on the feeding grounds and likely expending little energy. It is the later stages of pregnancy (third trimester) that come at a true cost, since this coincides with the time when baleen whales must travel vast distances while fasting, living for months on accumulated subcutaneous fat reserves in the blubber, muscle, and intra-abdominal fat deposits. But these whales have figured it out. As capital breeders, the cost of reproduction in the breeding grounds is covered by their stored energy, accumulated from feeding grounds thousands of miles away. It is what allows a Humpback, for example, to undertake their mind-boggling 10,000-mile (16,000-km) round trips—all while fasting.

This migration period undertaken by fasting pregnant baleen whales is sufficiently precarious and increasingly challenged by anthropogenic threats. Females in poor body condition will be more likely to abort their fetus during this third trimester, as indicated by the higher rates of miscarriage in the later stages of pregnancy in Fin Whales (*Balaenoptera physalus*). However, larger body

HUMPBACK WHALE MOTHER AND CALF
The journeys these pairs undertake together can be astonishingly long.

FIN WHALE
Female Fin Whales must build up fat reserves during early pregnancy to reduce the risk of miscarriage during migration.

size is thought to offer a buffer against disturbances, since it gives whales a greater ability to accumulate the energy reserves necessary to sustain them in the face of reduced food availability and fasting. In general, body size matters in mammals, as bigger mothers give birth to bigger offspring, and bigger mothers can also invest more in their offspring than smaller mothers.

BIRTH

As we all know, whales, being mammals, give birth to live young. These neonates, or newborns, are popped out into a watery world, presenting a host of challenges that require careful attention from the mother whale. The calves must immediately figure out how to stay warm, avoid predators, get to the surface to breathe, and, of course, avoid drowning.

Identifying and observing a neonate

Despite their great size, whale birth has rarely been documented in the wild and so we know very little about the early beginnings of most whale calves. However, some lucky observers have documented the births of Orcas (*Orcinus orca*), Sperm Whales, Belugas (*Delphinapterus leucas*), False Killer Whales (*Pseudorca crassidens*), Right Whales, and Gray Whales (*Eschrichtius robustus*), all of which have at least given us some insight into what happens during this critical period.

Research that looked at a series of Humpback births showed that two-thirds took place with at least one escort (an adult whale, typically not a male, who accompanies a female with a calf) present. The neonates were seen making a consistent tail-slapping movement (see page 82), sharks were documented scavenging on the placenta, and there was evidence of possible predation on the neonates, too. Females were often, but not always, observed supporting calves at the surface; however, temporary calf abandonment for less than 10 minutes at a time also occured. Interestingly, researchers also found that blood and placenta are not always evident from the surface, which means that even if a whale birth were occurring close to a boat, it would be easy for those on board to miss it.

While the Costa Rica Dome is a suspected birthing ground for Blue Whales, just two Blue Whale births have been recorded, with one from Saladanha Bay whaling station in South Africa in 1911 and the other in Trincomalee Harbor on the east coast of Sri Lanka in 1946, indicating that these, too, might be calving areas. In 2011, scientists observed the birth of a Humpback Whale calf in the coastal waters off Sainte Marie Island, Madagascar. The mother was surrounded throughout the process by 14 escorts who were likely focused on protecting her and her newborn calf. In 2023, a video of a Humpback Whale calf birth in Hawaii showed a female surrounded by 20 male escorts who slowed to a halt as she gave birth. They then supported her baby as it took its first-ever breath. In the same year, a video was recorded of a baby Sperm Whale being birthed off Dominica, where female social units roam. During the birth, the mother was surrounded by her sisters in a protective formation. They caressed her with their flippers and assisted by guiding the newborn to the surface for its first breath. These acts remind us that these social creatures are intelligent and empathetic.

Identifying a newborn calf can also be difficult. Curled tail flukes are considered a better characteristic for identifying neonates than fetal folds (skin creases

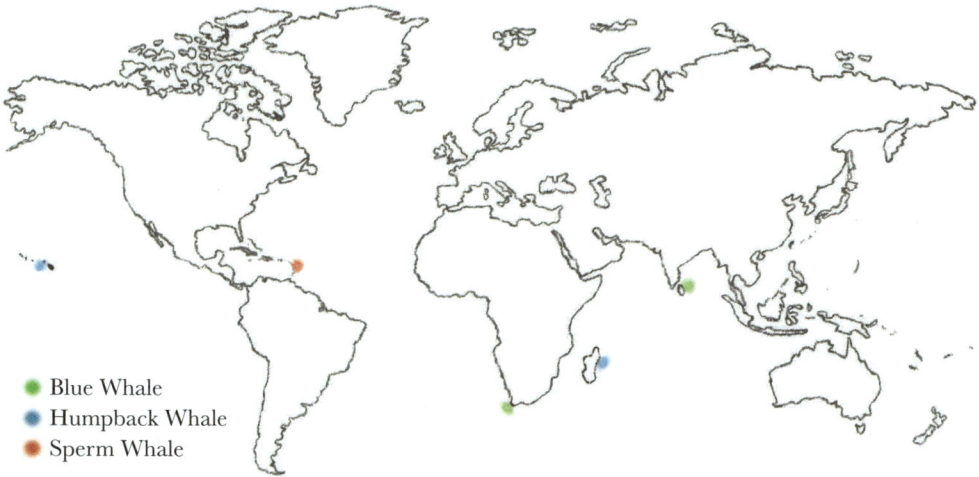

MAP OF KNOWN WHALE BIRTH LOCATIONS
*Blue Whale birth sites include Sri Lanka's Trincomalee Harbor and South Africa's
Saladanha Bay. Humpback births have been recorded in Saint Marie Island,
Madagascar, and Hawaii. A sperm whale birth has been recorded in Dominica.*

that appear on newborn dolphins due to their positioning in the womb)—which
are much less obvious. Furled fluke tips appear to be another feature of newborns, and have been noted in both Gray and Right Whales. Furled fluke tips are
accompanied by a furled dorsal fin, because in utero the fetus is bent like origami
and the dorsal fin is curled around the spine. The extreme flexibility of this dorsal
fin makes swimming difficult until it has stiffened and straightened out over the
first two weeks. This feature is useful for telling the relative age of a calf within a
breeding region. As the fin unfurls, its breath-hold capacity also increases.

While the newborn undergoes a series of changes during this period, so does
the mother. A Southern Right Whale mother's body volume is reduced by
about 1.6 times the birth volume of her newborn calf. This enormous loss,
which exceeds the birth volume of the calf, is likely due to the ejection of placenta and other tissues and fluids associated with fetal development during
birth. Over the next 20 days, the mother's body volume decreases further as she
invests heavily in the lactation phase of her reproductive cycle.

LACTATION

Lactation is extremely costly to new whale mothers. Once born, baby whales are fed some of the richest milk in the animal kingdom. In the absence of physical maternal support (no hands!), baby whales have to be able to suckle, swim, and hold their breath immediately after birth. Unlike in the terrestrial world, where suckling and its associated behaviors are easier to observe, little is known about suckling underwater. To ensure the mother whale remains hydrodynamically streamlined even when her breasts are full, the breasts are located deep under a layer of blubber on either side of her genital slit. Access is via two mammary slits—special folds of skin that enclose the feeding glands. When necessary, the nipples can be extruded from these slits for nursing.

Intense energy transfer

A mother Blue Whale gains nearly 50 tons (45,000 kg) during pregnancy, but has no trouble shedding this weight as she transfers it to her developing calf during lactation. At peak lactation, a nursing Blue Whale mother will produce about 50 gallons (190 l) of milk a day, and baleen whales in general will produce milk that has an average of 30–40 percent fat (compared to 4 percent in cow's milk), giving it the consistency of cream cheese or soft butter. As a side note, researchers studying Fin Whale milk describe it as having a viscous, creamy appearance but tasting slightly fishy when fresh and more like cod liver oil with an astringent kick when a bit older. Mother Blue Whales transfer about 4,000 megajoules, or nearly 1 million kilocalories, per day to their babies. Suckling Blue Whales gain around 10 lb (4.5 kg) an hour, or 250 lb (113 kg) a day! Since calves spend six to seven months suckling, their growth is rapid, going from 23 ft (7 m) in length at birth to 52 ft (16 m) by the age of six months.

Humpback Whale calves feed exclusively on their mother's milk for the first six months of life, after which they start to feed on "solids," or prey, in combination with milk, until weaning at 10–12 months old, in time for the mother to

BLUE WHALE MOTHER NURSING HER CALF
At peak lactation, a nursing Blue Whale mother will produce about 50 gallons of milk a day

return to the calving area. A Humpback Whale mother can lose up to 25–30 percent of her body weight during the nursing period, which equates to a weight loss of about 17–22 tons (15,000–20,000 kg), depending on her starting size. This loss is a result of energy transfer during lactation, when calves will ideally suckle for a fifth of their day. When they are able to suckle enough, the calves grow large; this is an asset in the open ocean since it provides an energetic advantage during migration and increases the probability of a calf surviving any predation events.

But not all whales produce milk in the same way. Baleen whales have an "intensive" strategy, producing high quantities of very high-fat milk over a short period, while toothed whales adopt an "extensive" strategy, producing lower-fat milk over longer periods of time. This makes sense in the grand scheme of things when you consider that baleen whales are capital breeders, feeding copiously before migrating to hang out on the nursery grounds where they feed little, if at all, and then returning to the feeding ground. Throughout this period they live off the blubber in their body. They have a short period on the nursery grounds, and in that time, they have to ensure that their calves are big and strong for the return journey.

Transferring fats and nutrients to the calves as fast as possible is a great strategy. Humpback Whale calves are said to grow 25–30 in (0.6–0.8 m) in length per month during this time.

Nursing safely

Suckling requires coordination between the mother and the calf. With Humpbacks, nursing happens between the sub-surface (<16 ½ ft/<5 m) and shallow depths (33–50 ft/10–15 m), or occasionally at the surface, where the mother will hold her tail in the air. The calf is then positioned vertically (head up, tail down) beneath the stationary mother but rolls continuously to the right when suckling on the right teat and vice versa. Calves alternate between nipples during suckling events. Dolphin calves, on the other hand, feed in motion, while swimming or gliding.

In many whales, like Humpback or Sperm Whales, nursing is initiated by tactile stimulation from the calf, which likely elicits an autonomic response that causes the extrusion of the nipple. Once extruded, the calf can then grasp the nipple with its tongue, which is lined with lingual papillae (fringes)

HUMPBACK WHALE CALF
Humpbacks grow incredibly quickly in their early months in preparation for the long migratory journeys they must undertake when still young.

that perhaps ensure the grasp is tight and the baby whale does not slip off. Once in position, the mother whale is thought to squeeze milk out of her nipple and into the mouth of the baby whale. A longer tongue would act as a straw for transferring milk from the nipple to the mouth of the waiting calf. However, Sperm Whales have an atypical short, stocky tongue that extends only to their last caudal teeth. To overcome the challenges posed by this anatomical feature, they stick their lower jaw (which still has no teeth) into the mother's genital slit (Belugas do this too) which gives them easier access to the mammary slits nearby. They are then able to use their tongues on the nipples. Mechanical, tactile cues are common among Bottlenose Dolphins (*Tursiops* sp.), Orcas, Sperm Whales, and Southern Right Whales, with Southern Right Whale calves sometimes head-butting their mothers if their request to suckle is rejected. Perhaps this silent form of communication prevents the mother–calf pair from attracting unwanted eavesdroppers.

MOTHER AND CALF

As soon as a baby whale is born, the mother gently nudges her calf's wobbly, awkward body to the surface, so they can take their first breath. During the first few weeks of a Southern Right Whale calf's life, it remains in constant close proximity to its mother. Such behavior has also been observed in species like Gray Whales, where the newborn swims at the peduncle of the mother, in Belugas, where the calf swims by the mother's fluke, and, in Humpbacks, where the calf often swims in front of or on the side of the mother. In time, and as calves get bigger and presumably more confident, they stray further away on their own accord.

In other mammal species, newborns are typically good sleepers, often taking time to rest and recover soon after birth. This focus on sleeping and feeding has been touted as important to proper development. With time, these periods of rest decrease as the young grow to adulthood and require less sleep. Unfortunately, for whales, things are quite different. Baby Orcas, Bottlenose Dolphins, and their mothers show little to no typical sleep behavior for the entire first month post-birth, focusing instead on avoiding obstacles and remaining mobile 24 hours a day. Periods of rest increase gradually, reaching healthy adult levels over a few months, but at no point does it exceed this.

Interestingly, whale and dolphin calves rest, eat, and sleep while their mothers swim by, tucking into the mother's mid-lateral flank and sliding into her slipstream. This is known as an echelon formation and is considered to be a form of "infant carrying" behavior. The calf enjoys the hydrodynamic benefits that enable proximity to their traveling mothers, but there is a cost: the mother's decreased locomotor performance and increased locomotor effort, as shown in Bottlenose Dolphins. Humpback Whale mothers modify their dive durations on foraging grounds to accommodate their calves' limited diving capabilities. This allows the calves to stay close and protected but also to have access to their mother's supply of milk.

MOTHER AND CALF IN ECHELON FORMATION
A common form of "infant carrying" in the whale world.

Communication and staying safe

Mother–calf pairs of Humpback Whales have been recorded "whispering" to one another using squeaky or grunting sounds that can be heard no more than 330 ft (100 m) away. They are very unlike the typical haunting sounds of communicating adult Humpbacks. These "whispers" are presumably to avoid attracting any unwanted attention: from nearby Orcas who love a good whale calf feast, or from Humpback male escorts that might be hovering in hopes of mating (and which could separate the mother–calf pair). These calls are used when traveling, perhaps as a way for the mother whale to keep track of her babbling baby. Worryingly, if noise pollution from ships, boats, and other sources of ocean noise continues to increase, the distances over which these quiet calls can travel will be reduced, increasing the risk of mother–calf separation.

Despite attempts to conceal newborns, wherever there are calves, there will be predators—Orcas, Short-finned Pilot Whales (*Globicephala macrorhynchus*), and False Killer Whales. To fend off attacks on their calves, Gray Whale mothers are known to lash at predatory Orcas with their fins and flukes, and to guide their offspring into shallower waters or kelp beds, hugging the coastline to avoid attack. In the event of an attack in which Orcas try to drown a calf, the mother is often seen nudging the calf to the surface repeatedly to ensure breathing continues. Sometimes, she might roll on her back while holding the calf up on her belly in an effort to protect it.

The calves also have to learn to protect themselves; this means holding their breath for increasingly long periods, and diving deeper and deeper over time. In the early months, calves stay near the surface and make only short, shallow dives, relying on their mother's guidance to gradually build diving skills. As they grow stronger and develop better lung capacity, the calves are often led by their mothers on progressively deeper dives, which helps the calves build endurance and adapt to the pressures of deeper water. This learning process is essential, as deep-diving skills are critical for foraging and to avoid predators.

Calf rest, movement, and play

Whale behavior develops with age, typically increasing the chance of survival as they become better equipped to face the challenges of the world, whether through learning to forage and hunt, or strengthening social bonds. Humpback calves on the calving ground are either in motion—practicing swimming or learning to breach—or stationary—resting or nursing. Metabolic costs in adult whales represent 40 percent maintenance and 60 percent locomotion, indicating that switching from travel to rest conserves energy in both mother and calf. This is particularly important because both mother and calf depend on the mother's built-up energy stores for the entirety of their time on the calving ground and over the return migration to their feeding grounds. If a calf is less active, more energy can be invested in growth, which is important for preparing for the upcoming migration and fending off predators.

Despite these constraints of a finite energy supply, surface activity is common among calves of all ages. Considered "play," this activity is important for developing motor skills and maneuverability. For example, "twirling," where the calf rotates 360 degrees around its long axis, is likely a useful antipredator behavior. In the face of an attack from Orcas, Humpbacks are often seen rolling as a means of defense—to protect their undersides. Calf tail slapping, tail swishing, and pectoral fin slapping are further common defense mechanisms in the face of Orcas. The ability to breath-hold for longer periods ensures a lower likelihood of drowning in the face of a predatory attack.

Like many newborn whale species, Southern Right Whales display a distinctive pattern of activity immediately after birth, followed by a period of rest. This period is crucial for their survival, ensuring they establish breathing, mobility, and maternal bonding. During the period of rest, they focus on conserving energy for growth by reducing movement and nursing frequently. These phases are reversed in Gray Whales. In the early stages, Gray Whales rest and nurse in calm waters, particularly in Mexico's San Ignacio Lagoon. This is then followed by a more active stage, with a shift to deeper waters where currents are stronger, and forays outside the breeding lagoons.

Many species of whales and dolphins appear to engage in forms of play. Orcas, Humpback, Right (both North Atlantic and Southern) and Gray Whales are often seen dragging kelp on any body part; often, they try to position the kelp in the notch of their flukes in a behavior known as kelping. Dolphins have been observed playing with pufferfish, sometimes even passing them around and gently chewing them, potentially to experience a mild narcotic effect from the pufferfish's toxins. I have also watched Striped Dolphins gently nudging and playing with pyrosomes, colonial tunicates, before taking a bite. What purpose these behaviors serve is yet unclear, but play plays a vital role in all species.

Growing up

The changes in diet, habitat, and social behaviors that an organism exhibits as it grows from birth to adulthood are known as ontogenetic shifts. They are often vital for a species' long-term survival, as shown with many types of whales. An example can be seen in the Pacific Coast Feeding Group (PCFG) of Gray Whales, a subgroup of the Eastern North Pacific population of Gray Whales. They forage in shallow coastal waters off northern California and southern British Columbia. This population has shown a clear ontogenetic shift in foraging tactic use, which appears to be related to increasing body length. They have been seen "headstanding," where an individual holds its large body in place, head down and tail up, while sculling its pectoral fins and beating its fluke to maintain position. This activity likely depends on body length and physical abilities like maneuverability, with very young whales likely unable to headstand. Generally, this behavior is more common in whales with greater body length and in greater depths of water, and is particularly common in reef habitats. Side-swimming (where a whale swims on its side but does not move forward) was particularly useful in this species group as it increased suction efficiency in these benthic feeders and helped conserve energy, and was evident among bigger whales, allowing them to feed more efficiently with minimal effort. Clearly, some tactics are only valuable up to a certain age and body length, after which they are replaced by more useful behaviors.

Grief and loss

Such are the bonds between mothers and calves that loss results in what some have interpreted as grief. Tahlequah, a southern resident Orca, gained renown in

AN INCREASINGLY RARE SIGHT
The birth rate of southern resident Orcas has dropped dramatically in recent years.

2018 when she carried her stillborn calf by balancing it on her head and rostrum or holding it in her mouth for 17 days around the Salish Sea, just off the coast of Washington, USA, and British Columbia, Canada. During this time, she may have traveled up to 1,000 miles (1,600 km). While there was much celebration when she was seen with a newborn calf swimming by her side in the latter part of 2024, it was sadly not to last. A few days later, the carcass of the newborn, who had suspected health issues, was again seen being carried around by Tahlequah. Given that the southern resident Orca population is endangered, any loss is a tremendous blow, particularly that of two female calves, given that there are now only an estimated 23 breeding females within this population.

While this example was followed intently by people across the world, it is by no means an isolated incident. Adult Indo-Pacific Bottlenose Dolphins (*Tursiops aduncus*), Atlantic Spotted Dolphins (*Stenella frontalis*), Spinner Dolphins (*Stenella longirostris*), Australian Humpback Dolphins (*Sousa sahulensis*), and Sperm Whales in some instances, have all been observed carrying dead calves or juveniles for an extended time after the youngster's death. These examples may indicate that grieving is part of being a highly social animal. These species typically live in close proximity in matrilineal groups throughout their lives—sometimes for as many as 60 years.

It takes a village

Alloparental care—care for a calf by a whale that is not the calf's biological mother—is widespread among toothed whales, including Beluga Whales, Bottlenose Dolphins, Spinner Dolphins, Orcas, and Pilot Whales. Sperm Whales, for example, often care for calves that are not their own, either while the mother dives deep or to protect them from predators.

In the presence of a predator, Sperm Whales also use what is thought of as the classic Sperm-Whale defensive formation—the rosette, wagon wheel, or "marguerite"—a form of communal defense that allows equal exposure to

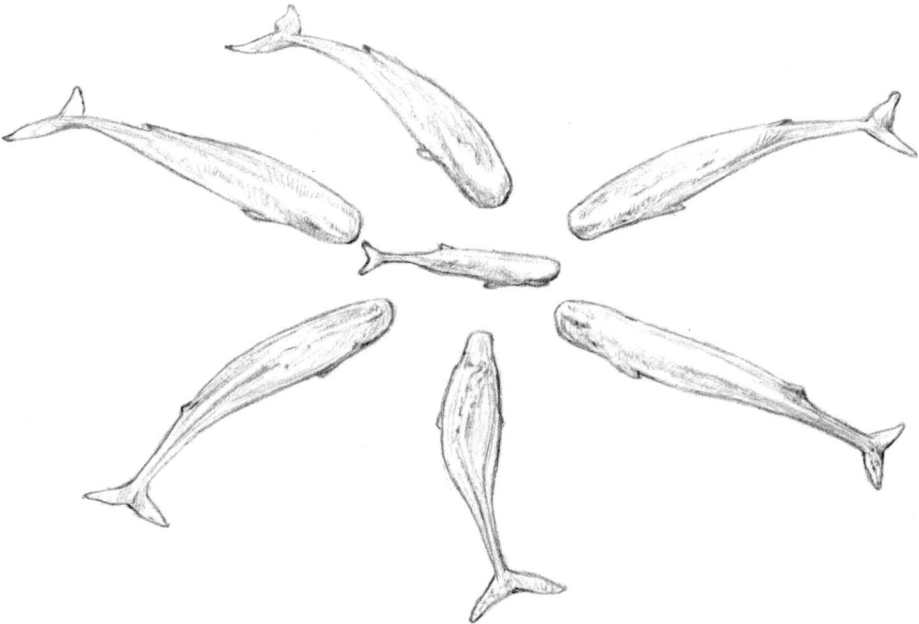

MARGUERITE FORMATION
Sperm Whales are known to adopt this communal defensive measure when under attack.

each individual in the group and limits the attack on the targeted individual (calf or injured young) who is placed at the center of the formation as the adults bring their heads together with their tails facing outward. In this formation, considered a "fight" response, it is thought that the whales are able to use their tails to slap at the attackers should they try to approach. As it turns out, this behavior is not exclusive to Sperm Whales but has also been displayed by Humpback, North Atlantic and Southern Right Whales in the face of danger.

Allonursing, where an individual lactates to feed a non-related calf, has been documented in wild Sperm Whale populations and captive Beluga and Bottlenose populations, but hasn't been reported among baleen whales. Older females typically carry out the nursing, which reduces the energy demands on the mother whale, who can focus on allocating resources to future offspring.

5

MAKING THEIR
WAY IN THE
WORLD

SOCIAL SYSTEMS

Whale social systems are complex and diverse, with a wide range of behaviors and structures that vary significantly between species. These systems can range from solitary individuals to intricate, stable matrilineal groups, and even to fluid, dynamic fission–fusion societies. Each type of social system has evolved to meet the specific needs of the species and offers distinct advantages, whether for foraging, mating, or protection. The diversity of social structures among whales reflects their adaptability to different environmental conditions, social dynamics, and evolutionary pressures. While some whale species prefer solitude, others form close-knit family units that last for generations. Additionally, species like Orcas (*Orcinus orca*) exhibit highly complex social networks that allow them to engage in cooperative hunting and share cultural behaviors. In contrast, some species, like Humpback Whales (*Megaptera novaeangliae*), form temporary groups during specific times of the year, such as during breeding or feeding seasons. Whale social systems are as varied as the species themselves, each playing a key role in the survival and success of these majestic marine mammals.

Sperm Whale connections

Sperm Whales (*Physeter macrocephalus*) live incredibly social lives. They communicate through clicks, patterned or otherwise, and touch. If you ever have the good fortune to come upon a maternal group of Sperm Whales, it is in your best interest to sit quietly and watch. They rub against each other and gently touch and nudge their young around—in fact, putting suction cup tags on Sperm Whales to collect behavioral data about their underwater lives can be particularly challenging because their constant rubbing can dislodge the tags! What is clear is that communication in these Sperm Whale populations is important—it keeps families together and helps expand families, as the whales use sound to find mates.

Sperm Whales live in matrilineal groups. Its "females females females" and a few young males—typically calves and juveniles. Once the young males reach a certain age and hit sexual maturity, they head off on their own. They go to cooler waters in search of greener pastures. They feed three times as much as female Sperm Whales, which are confined to the tropics, where productivity is lower. The roaming males are important because that is how they ensure their DNA is mixed as they seek and mate with females from other pods.

This might sound vaguely familiar to those enraptured by tropical terrestrial giants, because elephants have a similar social system. Both Sperm Whales and elephants are among the largest in their categories—Sperm Whales being the largest toothed whales and among the largest marine mammals, and elephants being the largest land mammals. They both possess the largest brains of any land or sea animal (typical of highly social beasts that engage in complex behaviors), and both Sperm Whales and elephants have complex social organizations—the females live in highly social family units that depend on well-developed communication systems. They are matrilineal in nature, with each family comprising grandmothers, their daughters, and offspring. A matriarch leads each group. When under attack, both groups take on a defensive formation.

Males, on the other hand, mature and then head out on their own. Sometimes, they catch up with loosely knit bachelor groups, but generally, they do their own thing, returning only during the breeding season. When they are ready to mate, they use specific advertisement calls; Sperm Whales use loud clangs, while elephants use "musth rumbles" to let the ladies know they have arrived and are available for mating.

In Sri Lanka, elephants roam the jungles while sperm whales roam the seas. They are an incredible example of convergent evolution: species that are not similar but that evolve similar behaviors independently—and while they live as neighbors, they may never know that each other exist.

Northern Bottlenose Whales (*Hyperoodon ampullatus*) grow to about 26 ft (8 m) long and have both a beak and a rounded head. Some researchers describe them as looking like Bottlenose Dolphins (*Tursiops sp.)* on steroids. Like Sperm Whales, they are deep divers and very social, though not matrilineal. Based on their similarities, researchers assumed they would have evolved similar characteristics and might have displayed the same signs of culture as those seen in Sperm Whales. As it turns out, the females maintain a looser network of friends while males form

NORTHERN BOTTLENOSE WHALE
A particularly social species of whale.

tighter alliances—which is more like Bottlenose Dolphin social systems. It goes to show, therefore, that a common environment alone does not drive convergence and that it is more complex than we might think.

Orcas—Mummy's boys

Young male Orcas, on the other hand, behave quite differently to Sperm and Northern Bottlenose Whales, despite also living in matrilineal groups. When Orca males mature, they search for a partner with whom they mate and return to their mother's pod almost immediately. Mother resident Orcas (one of three ecotypes found in the Pacific Northwest of North America) dote on their adult sons throughout their lives, which is perhaps the incentive to return. Essentially, these fathers invest very little in the growth of their own offspring, and the mothers are left with all the calf-rearing duties. Fortunately, she is supported by the other females in her pod.

On a regular day, males typically trail behind their mothers, grabbing bits of fish and food,while their sisters are not included in prey sharing; instead, the sisters give birth and look after their own calves. Moreover, postmenopausal Orca mothers are known to protect their sons from bullying and injuries inflicted by other Orcas, as is evidenced by the lack of tooth rake marks on their bodies. This protection is not, however, extended to the mother's daughters or grandchildren. It is hard not to wonder if the males appreciate their mothers intervening in their "school-ground" fights and fending off their bullies for them! Such behavior is probably because males can breed with multiple females, allowing them to produce more offspring than females—thus, the mother's investment in her son leads to the spread of her own genes.

Alliance formation and reproductive success

In Shark Bay, Western Australia, Bottlenose Dolphins display intense social behaviors such as cooperative hunting, and social play. So much so that after

A POD OF ORCAS
Such groups are typically led by females, who rear their own children, but also their grandchildren and even the offspring of their fellow pod members.

a disagreement, they are often seen petting and gently rubbing one another to repair their social bonds. These dolphins also organize into the most complex multi-level alliance networks—which form among similar-age males in their early to mid-teens—seen outside humans. Building long-term cooperative relationships and allyships has been important for the success of human society but is not unique to us. In the case of the Shark Bay dolphins, cooperative relationships are important for increasing male access to a contested resource—females.

First-order alliances constitute stable pairs and trios of males that cooperate to aggressively herd individual females that are sexually receptive or in estrus, the period in the reproductive cycle when female mammals are sexually receptive and capable of mating, controlling their movements over periods of days to weeks. Males make an audible "popping" vocalization to encourage the female to approach, and if she misses that hint, he resorts to threatening or attacking her. Herded females routinely try to bolt, but the alliance of males

SHARK BAY DOLPHIN
The highly intelligent Bottlenose Dolphins of Shark Bay, Western Australia,
live within complex and mutually beneficial societies.

often triangulate around her while swimming, preventing her from being able to escape in any direction. If the female miraculously escaped, the herding would end, but the alliance would not.

Second-order alliances form when first-order alliances combine, resulting in 4–14 unrelated males swimming together. These stable alliances form the core unit of male social organization, with males moving synchronously (in unison). Their primary function? Competing for and stealing females from other first-order alliances. Third-order intergroup alliances form between two or more cooperating second-order alliances. The cooperative relationships between groups allow them to spend more time with females by providing mutual protection and suppressing competition. As they then spend more time with sexually receptive females, they can ensure they can mate and increase their opportunities for reproductive success. While Bottlenose Dolphins in Sarasota Bay, off Florida, also form alliances, they are much less complex than those found in Shark Bay.

MATING

Whales are incredibly large but they are simply needles in the haystack of the ocean's vastness. Despite their size, we know little about their mating habits, and there is still so much we have to learn and witness about their lives.

Humpback Whale mating behavior

Despite their popularity and general showiness (be that through breaching or pectoral fin slapping), Humpback Whales (*Megaptera novaeangliae*) have kept the sexual aspect of their lives firmly under wraps for a very long time. However, on an expedition in the Dominican Republic, I managed to watch a single female Humpback Whale engaging with multiple competitive groups of males over the course of a few days. On the first occasion, she kept rolling around, displaying herself in a group of six males. One particular male, who clearly had a keener interest in her than the rest, gently swam under her while exhaling bubbles through his blowholes. This happened not once, or twice but repeatedly over the course of a couple of hours. Perhaps this was a courtship ritual and him establishing that she was his. All the while, the other males swam around but did not interfere with this gentle moment. She did not seem in any hurry to leave, so we left cheering for the apparently victorious male that had invested so heavily in charming her that it appeared he could not lose.

However, a day or two later, we found her in the midst of another competitive group. This time, 11 males fighting for her fancy. The first part of the courtship began with the males swimming fast behind her while body-slamming and shoving each other out of the way. Eventually, one of them "won" and was spotted swimming by the female. It is fascinating to think about this act of flirtation, which may or may not have amounted to promiscuity. It was clear that the female was in charge of choosing her mate and that she was not in any hurry to make this important decision, given that she was on the lookout for the fittest father for her future calf. While we do not know which one she picked or if she picked any at all, we left very invested in her act of choice.

In fact, until 2022, no one had ever witnessed Humpback Whales mating. Then, one day, two photographers noticed two whales swimming slowly toward their boat, off the coast of the Hawaiian Island of Maui. They stopped to investigate, and it turned out that one whale would approach the other from behind, hang on with its pectoral flippers and copulate, each copulation taking just two minutes. This observation, while rather voyeuristic, was exciting for the entire scientific community. The first documentation of Humpback Whales having sex was not something to ignore.

When the photographers showed their photos to a local scientist, everyone was in for an even bigger surprise. As it turned out, the two whales were known by the scientists, who identified them both as sexually mature males, with the one in front being 13 years old and the one at the back being 30 years old. What a plot twist! Homosexual behavior is actually quite common in the animal kingdom. Within the cetacean world, it has been documented in several species, including

Common Bottlenose Dolphins (*Tursiops truncatus*), Atlantic Spotted Dolphins (*Stenella frontalis*), Amazon River Dolphins (*Inia geoffrensis*), Orcas, Gray Whales (*Eschrichtius robustus*), and Bowhead Whales (*Balaena mysticetus*).

Slow and steady wins the race

One of my favorite documentary scenes is from BBC's *Life of Mammals*, narrated by Sir David Attenborough. In it, he walks us through a chaotic scene involving a female Southern Right Whale (*Eubalaena australis*) and several males desperately trying to become the father of her next born off the coast of Patagonia, Argentina. The males signal their arrival by breaching and engaging in behaviors that make them hard to miss. The female, unprepared for the mating that will ensue, rolls on her back to protect her genitals from penetration.

This does not stop the males, however, as they approach her and release their 12-ft (3.7-m) long, incredibly flexible penises out of their genital slits, where they typically remain sheathed to prevent them from dangling around and potentially increasing drag by making the whale's body less streamlined. Once out, these penises look like they have a mind of their own as they snake their way in the direction of the female's underside in search of her genital slit and an opportunity to penetrate her. Not one, but many males proceed to do this. It is worth keeping in mind that Southern Right Whale males have the largest testes in the world, each weighing more than 157 stone and filled with gallons of sperm—this is indicative of their promiscuity. In this scene, the female continues to remain on her back but the males are relentless. Finally, she decides that it is time—she rights herself (no pun intended) and, as she does so, other males approach her and also take their chance. However, they each have so much sperm that, with each ejaculation, they flush out the sperm of her previous suitor. This is a process called sperm competition, where multiple males mate with a female and the sperm of the different males compete to fertilize the female's eggs. It is a strategy used by other species such as Bowhead Whales and Gray Whales. In the end, the male that has the higher chance of winning, is the male that patiently remains until the end.

Unique dolphin anatomy

In the wild, dolphin sex feels very much like a "blink and you miss it" type of event. But the more you dive in, the more complex you realize it all is. Dusky (*Lagenorhynchus obscurus*) and Spinner Dolphins (*Stenella longirostris*) will turn belly-to-belly for a split second and then return to what they were doing. Harbor Porpoises (*Phocoena phocoena*) might be small, but their penises are large—almost the length of their bodies—and their copulation is rather dramatic. The male will wait for the female to come to the surface of the water to take a breath and then he will leap out of the water and try to hook her with his penis. Bottlenose Dolphins are promiscuous, with the female mating with many males. To do this, they make a T-formation where the male crosses the female exactly at her midline. The female's vagina is a convoluted maze made up of intricate folds and flaps that the male's penis must navigate if he is to deposit his sperm within range of her eggs. How he manages to aim, fire, and hit the bullseye in mere seconds is unclear, but it is thought that

Penis envy?

My only encounter with a whale penis, which I recognize is not something most people ever have, was at the Explorers Club in New York in 2018. It so happened that I was at an awards ceremony, staring at what could easily be mistaken for a sorting hat. However, it was a stuffed Sperm Whale penis mounted on an oak base sitting unabashedly, pointing skyward. While the Explorers Club is home to many taxidermized specimens, this one was, as you can imagine, the most surprising. More surprising is how it got to the club. As it turns out, in 1977, Mr. and Mrs. Frederick S. Schauffler were so regretful that they missed the whaling exhibition being hosted at the club that they penned a note, packed it with this whale appendage gift, and had it dropped off.

SPINNER DOLPHIN
Mating between Spinner Dolphins is a belly-to-belly affair.

the complexity of her vagina is intentional. Suppose the female does not want to mate with a particular male. In that case, she can shift her body slightly so that his penis hits one of the convolutions in her vaginal labyrinth so that his ejaculation takes longer to get to her eggs and may result in unsuccessful copulation.

While every dolphin mating encounter I have ever witnessed (yes, I have been quite lucky) has been incredibly rapid, with males and females coming together for a split second of copulation and then going their separate ways, a recent encounter has given me more insight into the process. In this scenario, we had 14 Spinner Dolphins that did not seem to be in any hurry to get anywhere. Their focus? Mating. I watched their pre-mating behaviours with interest-flipper rubbing, body touching, nudging, and gently poking or biting the genital slit with their beaks. I cannot be sure that it was the males instigating this, but in Brazil's Fernando de Noronha archipelago, these behaviors have been associated with the males. Following the pre-mating rituals, a male would approach the female from the underside and latch on. I knew which one was a male because I could see the tip of his penis even after they had separated. Even if she sped up, he would stick with her. As she rose to the surface to breathe, he was still there. This took about 10 seconds each time. Dolphins are also notoriously promiscuous, so some definite mate swapping also happened.

I will say, with all my years on the ocean observing these species, this was one of the most exciting things I have ever witnessed.

Interestingly, dolphins have sex year-round, even when they are not ready to get pregnant and have babies, leaving researchers hypothesizing about what the purpose of it all might be. Non-reproductive sexual behaviors (including same-sex mating) potentially have a range of purposes, including providing opportunities to practice for future sexual encounters and opportunities, providing an opportunity for establishing or maintaining a relationship between individuals, or asserting dominance. Bottlenose Dolphin anatomy also suggests that sex is pleasurable, which makes sense, as the more fun it is, the more individuals will seek out sex, increasing opportunities for reproductive success.

Hybridization between species

Hybrids are only possible between two genetically distinct species that have overlapping ranges and have some common morphological and behavioral traits, such as body length or vocalization frequency. For example, mules are the result of a cross between a male donkey and a female horse. In most cases, if hybridization is possible, the hybrid offspring are sterile or infertile and unable to give birth to young themselves. This might happen if the mixed chromosomes of the hybrid embryo do not match up properly or carry a complete set of information.

Hybridization between two species has been documented more frequently among bird species but less so among terrestrial species. In the cetacean world, hybridization has been documented in about 20 percent of species, both in captivity and the wild, with most crosses occurring between dolphin species. Many of these matings give rise to viable hybrid offspring, which hints at the fact that in most cetaceans, postmating barriers to inbreeding are incomplete. The key thing is that cetaceans do not have defined territories; they roam freely within and across ocean basins and live in social groups. While social groups are great for increasing your success at capturing prey or fending off predators, they lead to a higher rate of parasitism and disease at inbreeding than those individuals that might live solitarily. If species travel in mixed species groups, then, the opportunity for interspecific hybridization increases.

Fin and Blue Whale hybridization

The two largest species on our planet have also been found to join forces to produce hybrid offspring, not once but many times over. However, we still believe the documented cases are underestimated because large whales are elusive, and it is tricky to identify hybrids purely based on looks (though historically, morphological features were all that were available for distinguishing hybrids from purebreds—but this required close inspection of carcasses). The first-ever Fin (*Balaenoptera physalus*) and Blue Whale (*Balaenoptera musculus*) hybrid was caught and documented as far back as 1887, off the coast of Lapland. Called "bastards" by whalers, others have since been reported, including: in 1965 off Kodiak Island, Alaska; and in 1983, 1986, and 1989 in Icelandic waters. In 1984, off the coast of northwest Spain, a female hybrid was caught by whalers, who described an animal with Fin Whale coloration and proportions but which was much larger in size. In 2013 and 2018, two hybrids were also caught off the coast of Iceland and one living hybrid is known to have visited northeast Iceland's Skjálfandi Bay almost annually since 2012.

In most cases (bar one in 1983 which was the offspring off a Fin Whale mother and Blue Whale father), the cross occurred between a Blue Whale mother and a Fin Whale father, providing evidence that hybridization is unidirectional, particu-

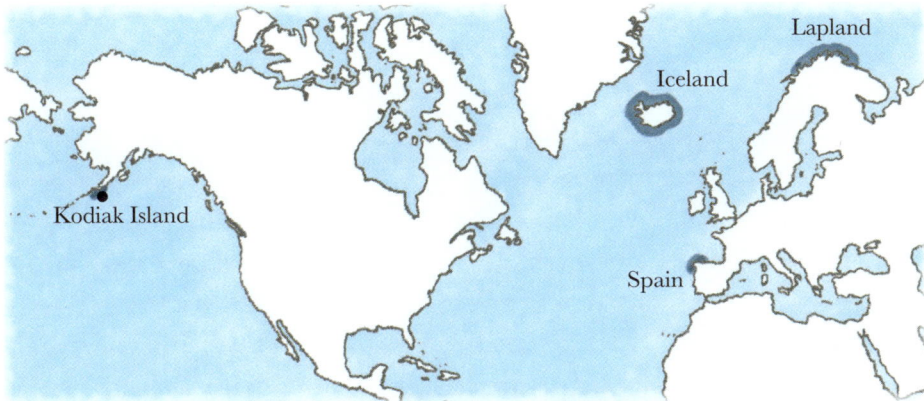

WHALE HYBRIDS
Blue Whale-Fin Whale hybrids have been documented in a few places around the world, including around the Scandinavian mainland, Iceland and Alaska.

larly in the Icelandic population. This particular combination finds support in the "sexual selection hypothesis for unidirectional hybridization," where it is thought that females of a species that are lower in numbers, or rarer, will mate with males of a more abundant species because of the lack of conspecifics to mate with.

An alternate hypothesis suggests that size-related limitations determine which species the male and female will be, because the larger species would be hard-pressed to successfully mate with females of the smaller species, particularly when you consider the Blue Whale–Fin Whale combo. However, given the propensity of hybrids in Icelandic waters, where disproportionate population sizes have been documented (the North Atlantic central region, where most of these hybrids have been recorded, is home to a Fin Whale population of approximately 36,800, while the Blue Whale population is ten times lower at 3,000 individuals), chances are that these hybrids occur as a result of the lack of a suitable, same-species mate to pair with.

Crossbreeding with hybrids

While hybrid offspring have often been thought to be infertile due to the cross occuring between genetically distinct species (as in the case of a mule—the offspring of a male donkey and female horse—or a hinnie—the offspring of a male horse and female donkey), in the whale world, there seem to be at least some exceptions to the rule. It appears that hybrids are able to back cross, where a hybrid offspring will mate with an individual of either parental species, with much success. The success of this was noted when a second-generation adult male hybrid was found to be the offspring of a female hybrid mother and pure Fin Whale father.

Common Minke Whales (*Balaenoptera acutorostrata*), cosmopolitan in distribution, and Antarctic Minke Whales (*B. bonaerensis*), found in the Southern Hemisphere, are two genetically distinct species, and the only other large whale species where hybridization has been documented. In 2010, a captured pregnant female was found to be the offspring of a female North Atlantic Common Minke Whale (*Balaenoptera acutorostrata acutorostrata*), a subspecies of the Common Minke, and an Antarctic Minke Whale male. The pregnancy was an indication of the fertility of this hybrid combination.

While hybridization is fascinating, it is not without its issues. When rarer species mate with more abundant species, there is a chance that genetic swamping might occur, where local genotypes may be replaced by that of the hybrids. This creates a veritable loss of the genetic pool of the rarer species, which threatens that species' persistence. While documentation of hybrids remains tricky, monitoring the number of individuals in a population is important to ensure that population numbers are not erroneously overestimated.

MENOPAUSE— REPRODUCTIVE SENESCENCE

In most species, females maximize their reproductive success by remaining reproductively capable throughout their adult lives. While humans are the only terrestrial mammal species to experience menopause, menopause has evolved multiple times among toothed whales. Short-finned Pilot Whales (*Globicephala macrorhynchus*), Orcas, False Killer Whales (*Pseudorca crassidens*), Narwhals (*Monodon monoceros*), and Belugas (*Delphinapterus leucas*) are some of the species known to live much beyond their reproductive lifespan. The big question, then, is what is the purpose of menopause in the lives of these marine wanderers? Why did it evolve?

A menopausal female Orca, often a grandmother, can live up to about 90 years in the wild, 20 of which are post-menopause. The advantage? The grandmother Orca's life overlaps with that of her offspring and grand-offspring. Her presence, along with that of the mother's, is known to result in the increased survival of their grand-offspring, particularly their adult sons. The death of older female resident Orcas was also said to compromise the survival of these two groups. Because the grandmother Orca is not distracted by her reproductive and related duties she can focus on the important tasks of knowledge transmission and hunting (of which grandmothers might do up to 90 percent).

Having an older female who can share knowledge and teach skills while helping hunt and find prey is valuable in many ways, doing all the important things a mother might not have time to do. Social learning is incredibly important for these species, with knowledge sharing coming from teaching and doing.

While the generational overlap is largely positive, it can result in harmful reproductive competition between mothers and daughters in any species where multiple generations are reproductively active at the same time. Living together and being able to support without competing for resources makes the menopause sound like something every species group should seek to evolve.

WHALES AND CULTURE

While most traits like eye color are passed on genetically through our nuclear DNA, some behaviors are learned through family members and friends. However, whether a community of runners chooses to wear the same T-shirt, or a group of friends chooses to use a handshake that is specific to them, is not engrained in our DNA, but is passed on through sharing, knowledge transfer, and learning. In many cases, birdsong is also not inherited but passed on through learning.

Cetaceans are predisposed to exhibit culture by virtue of their life-history traits, which include having long lives with prolonged parental care, large brains with advanced cognitive abilities, and complex social structures where the most basic element is the long-term social unit, or pod. The fact that whales are highly mobile and not territorial also makes culture in these species more ecologically and evolutionarily significant. Despite the logistical difficulties involved in studying cetacean culture, strong evidence supporting its presence comes from the observation of ethnographic patterns (patterns of variation not related to ecology or genetics) in Sperm Whales, Belugas, Orcas, and Bottlenose Dolphins. Past studies have shown that transmission of culture in this group occurs both vertically (learning from parents or other elders) and horizontally (learning from peers). Because vertical transmission is said to lead to cultures that are stable enough to support traditions in which information accumulates from one generation to the next, matrilineal species are expected to exhibit this form of cultural transmission.

Sperm Whale culture

Sperm Whales are organized into social units that comprise about ten females and their young. Grandmother, her daughters, and their daughters and young sons do everything together—traveling vast distances thanks to their nomadic lifestyles, communally caring for their young (with babysitting and wet nursing within the unit), and protecting their young together. Sperm Whales, which have the largest noses in the world, also produce the loudest noises on Earth— clicks that they use to find food—and when these sounds are organized into distinct patterns, they emerge as codas that are used for communication.

Each unit has a distinct repertoire of codas, which members of a few other units might use. This collection of units is called a vocal clan. In the Galápagos, where Sperm Whales have been studied for decades, the species is organized into two distinct vocal clans. The "regular" clan, where a series of clicks in a coda are regularly spaced, and the "+1" clan, where the clicks in a coda are regularly spaced up until the final click where there is an extended interval between clicks. These clans use the same waters but never interact. They are genetically the same but exhibit quite different behaviors. The "regular" clan stays close to shore and travels in squiggly paths, while the "+1" clan uses off-shore waters and travels in very straight lines.

The genetic similarity does not explain how two groups of the same species living in a shared habitat might be so different, but culture does. Their pre-ferred behaviors are socially transmitted from mother to calf—and this shared knowledge becomes a part of their culture.

This is a great reminder that two forms of inheritance give rise to the behaviors we see, each with its own transmission pathway. Genetically inher-ited traits are transmitted through sex, while culturally inherited traits are passed on through knowledge sharing either from parent to child (typically

POD OF SPERM WHALES
Sperm Whales are matriarchical, with pods comprising a grandmother, her daughters, and their offspring.

mother to calf, given that cetacean fathers are mostly absentee dads) or between peers. Not all species have culture, and, as far as we know, apart from a handful of cetacean species, culture has not been documented in the majority of cetacean species. That said, it might exist among more, but given how elusive and difficult to study whales are, we just may not have pinpointed it yet. But we do know that culture is vital to a species like the Sperm Whale. These whales' ability to survive depends on the passing on of information about where the best food sources are or where safe refuges might be.

DEATH

A dead whale is a feast to a range of species. At the surface, the carcass may be preyed on by sharks and gulls. En route to the bottom of the seafloor, other species will take bites, and when it finally settles on the bottom of the ocean as "whale fall," species like slimy hagfish, octopus, and zombie bone worms take over, boring and sucking at the bare bones lying on display. No part of the whale is spared, which means no part of the whale is wasted.

However, not all deaths are timely. Some happen prematurely, either because of a predatory attack, typically from Orcas, illness, as in the case of some stranding events, abandonment due to environmental or other forms of stress, or human causes like collisions with ships or entanglements with fishing gear.

Mass strandings deserve a particular mention. We often hear the sad news of hundreds of whales washing up alive on beaches, hopefully to be saved by volunteers but sometimes, sadly, to die. Strandings can even make euthanization necessary; if they remain outside of water for too long, whales' organs can be crushed under the weight of their body, making survival impossible. Pilot Whales (*Globicephala* sp.) are famously known to mass strand, but other species like False Killer Whales can also be affected. Why this happens remains a mystery because it is unethical to test the causes of such events. But theories exist. For instance, with highly social species, if one individual gets sick, injured, or disoriented, its pod might follow it onto shore and into danger. Similarly, if deep-water species follow their prey into shallower waters, and get caught in waves or struggle to echolocate, they may also be washed up. In some cases, particularly with beaked whales in the Bahamas, stranding events have been linked to military sonar exercises which can cause whales to ascend too fast and get "the bends," while yet others end up dying on beaches.

While Bowhead Whales are said to live for over a century, surprisingly little is known about the lifespans of other species. But many live longer than was once thought. Comparing the lifespans of the heavily hunted North Atlantic Right Whales with the thriving Southern Right Whales has shown that only 10 percent of the former live beyond 47 years while up to 10 percent of the latter live past 130 years. This long lifespan should come as no surprise given that body size is correlated with longevity and whales are the largest living organisms on earth. However, we are taken aback by these numbers because few animals in our waters today have the privilege of living out their full lifespans. Hunting is not the biggest threat faced by these species today; shipping and related maritime industries have taken that title. It is amazing to think that our oceans could be home to at least a small percentage of whales that survived decades of industrial whaling, either by luck or by learning. In other cases, premature deaths are inexplicable but happen, and are accompanied by visible displays of grief, as in the case of Tahlequah in the Salish Sea (see page 83). Either way, death is one of the few guarantees in life and, while heart-breaking, is a reminder of the fickleness of life.

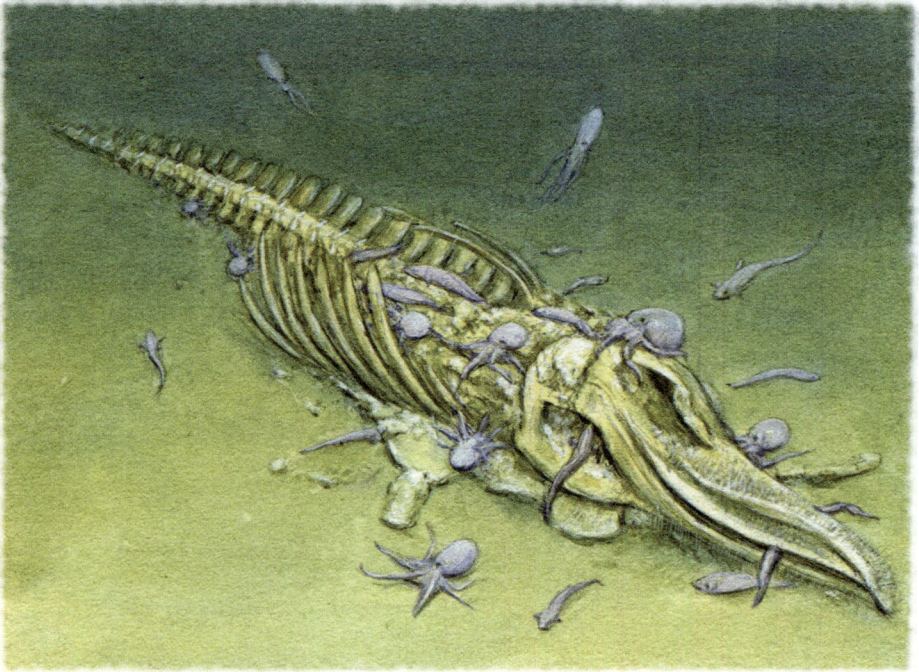

WHALE FALL
Dead whale carcasses fall slowly to the seafloor, and as they do, they serve as food for many species.

6

FEEDING AND HUNTING

FINDING FOOD

A species' survival depends on its access to resources, particularly food. While this food comes in many forms, its acquisition varies, depending on how dynamic or sedentary it might be. For example, many whales have grown into some of the biggest the planet has ever seen by exploiting tightly swarming species such as krill or shrimp, that do not swim away in the presence of a predator. This method of feeding requires them to expend less energy but requires them to be incredibly astute at finding dense prey patches that are worth lunging through to fulfill their daily nutritional needs. Sperm Whales (*Physeter macrocephalus*), on the other hand, are thought to wrestle giant squid at depth—with the winner either becoming dinner or living to fight another day. Imagine holding your breath in the deepest, darkest parts of the ocean, under pressure, and battling it out with a rather slippery suction-cupped giant?

GIANT SQUID
The Sperm Whale's greatest nemesis, and also one of its favorite foods.

Whales have learned to exploit a wide variety of marine animals, including tiny krill, bottom-dwelling fish, shrimp, seals, and even large cephalopods and other whales. To do this, they have embraced an equally wide range of unique hunting techniques, from blowing bubbles and putting sponges on their noses to simply opening their mouths wider than one would expect, all in order to get their recommended daily allowance of calories.

Much of what we know about whale hunting comes from close observation of the lives of Orcas, apex predators that have sophisticated and well-documented hunting methods. However, despite their ability to evolve incredible hunting strategies to suit the nature of their prey, changes in their environment largely caused by humans might result in them being caught short as prey supplies diminish.

Orcas' hunting techniques

In our modern-day food web, there are six trophic levels showing the position an organism occupies, with each level determining what eats what in an ecosystem. Orcas (*Orcinus orca*) sit comfortably at the top level, dominating their marine environment as the apex predator. They also display some of the most sophisticated hunting techniques of any animals on Earth. Like with many other species, their hunting behaviors are adapted to their habitat and prey. For example, resident Orcas teach their young how to catch salmon by showing them how to toss and play with young porpoises that are similar in size. Once proficient, they use these strategies in the real world, including slapping the fish with their tails to stun them.

COOPERATIVE HUNTING

In Norway, Orcas feed cooperatively using a form of cooperative hunting called carousel feeding, whereby they use a combination of air bubbles and belly flashes to herd herring into a tight ball close to the surface. The Orcas then slap the edge of the school of herrings with the underside of their tail flukes, picking off the stunned fish one by one. Common Bottlenose Dolphins (*Tursiops truncatus*) in the Black Sea have also been seen hunting using the carousel method.

COMMON BOTTLENOSE DOLPHIN
These intelligent hunters also use the carousel method to catch their prey.

Transient Orcas in the North Pacific, specifically off California, have realized the value of hunting in the open sea, where competition is less and food is abundant. Despite their prey often being many times their size, these Orcas are known to make a feast of northern elephant seals, Gray Whale (*Eschrichtius robustus*) calves, Minke Whales (*Balaenoptera acutorostrata*), sea lions, dolphins, and porpoises. Orcas in this area hunt Gray Whale calves using brute force—ramming their prey or slapping it with their tails up into the air before settling in for the feast. But to ensure that the hunt is worth the risk (which includes defensive mothers, injury, and the considerable time and energy that is expended in subduing the calves), the Orcas work in packs, typically of 15 or more. The pack initially work to separate the Gray Whale mother from the calf. The mother whale attempts to interpose between the Orcas and her calf, and slaps and thrashes with her tail to fend off the Orcas while guiding her calf toward the safety of shallower waters. The relentless Orcas ram and bite the calf and then swim atop it to drown it. The mother whale does not give up and swims under the calf to push it up to the surface to protect its vulnerable belly and throat and ensure it can continue to breathe. If the calf begins to tire and the mother's defenses drop, it is then that the Orcas will seize the advantage, kill the calf, and begin to feast.

The Orcas typically spend up to 12 hours feeding on a single calf, perhaps indicating that the calf provides a considerable mass of food. Not only do they feed on the submandibular sac and tongue, but they have also been seen feeding on chunks of blubber from other parts of the calves' bodies—indicating that little goes to waste. While big groups mean smaller shares on the whole, they also make it easier to defeat Gray Whale calves, not least due to a bigger pool of hunting skills. Large groups may also allow the Orcas to better protect the carcasses from scavenging sharks. In Alaska's Aleutian Islands, Orcas are known to prolong feeding on a Gray Whale carcass by storing it in shallow water—the Orca equivalent of a fridge—where they can return to it to remove chunks of blubber and muscle tissue as needed.

CLEVER ORCA ADAPTATIONS

As it turns out, no prey is too big for Orcas. Since 2019, Orca pods off Bremer Bay, Western Australia, have been documented hunting the largest animal on earth—the Blue Whale (*Balaenoptera musculus*). Each attack was led by a female Orca of the pod, with the entire pod seen gathering, biting, and ramming the Blue Whale relentlessly, with some pushing its head underwater. Before the Blue Whale dies, an Orca will swim inside its mouth to retrieve the nutritionally dense tongue of the flailing beast. In one incident, where a Blue Whale calf was attacked and its tongue consumed, about 50 Orcas swam by, bringing up large chunks of flesh to the surface and sharing in the feast. Most Orca populations are fussy eaters, specializing only in certain types of prey, but Orcas off Bremer Bay have a particularly diverse diet, which even includes elusive deep-diving beaked whales.

Orcas also indulge in coordinated attacks on prey relaxing on ice floes. They charge the ice floe in tight formation, creating a huge wave front that makes the prey, often a seal, unstable, knocking it right off its safe haven. Just before reaching the ice floe, the Orcas dive and use their tails to give one last push to sweep the seals off their comfortable perch. The imagery of these encounters clearly conveys the emotions of the seals in their last moments—their eyes turn into veritable dinner plates, fear filling every corner as they slide into the ocean knowing their chances of survival are slim.

Along the sharply sloping beaches of Punta Norte in Argentina's Patagonia region, Orcas sometimes even ride waves up the beach, swimming sideways to camouflage their tell-tale dorsal fins. Amazingly, they then beach themselves to get within reach of sea lion pups, which they grab with their teeth. While beaches are typically death traps for whales and dolphins, these Orcas have mastered the art of maneuvering back into the water through a combination of hopping and sliding motions. This unusual behavior was displayed exclusively by two Orca families in the Southern Hemisphere and is socially transmitted from mother to offspring. However, more recently, Orcas off Protection Island in the Salish Sea have also been documented beaching themselves in favor of a morsel. Here, instead of grabbing their prey while stranding themselves, the Orcas scare the seal pups into the water, where they become easy pickings. This may indicate that the behavior is still at its earliest stages of evolution, and perhaps, some day in the not-too-distant future, these Orcas will also be beaching themselves for the chance of a meal.

ORCA ATTACK
Orcas encircling an unsuspecting seal relaxing on an ice floe.

SEA LION PUP
Orcas in Punta Norte, Argentina, beach themselves in pursuit of sea lion young.

TROPICAL AND SUBTROPICAL ORCA AND SPERM WHALE BATTLES

In Sri Lanka, a tropical population of Orcas roam the oceans. While there is still much to learn about them, what is clear is that they have a penchant for whales. In 2013, a pod of Orcas was seen and documented launching an attack on a pod of Sperm Whales, which included one calf. The adult Sperm Whales immediately assumed the "marguerite," or wagon wheel, formation, bringing their heads together in the center with their tails facing outward like the spokes of a wheel. The vulnerable calf was positioned in the center of the formation, and the adults slashed their tails back and forth to ward off the Orcas coming in for a bite. The Sperm Whales were successful in defending their calf, forcing the Orcas to retreat.

Orca predation on Sperm Whales has also been documented in the Pacific off California. The encounters are brutal, with pods of Sperm Whales being outnumbered and taken down by pods of Orca. Again, Sperm Whales would assume the marguerite formation as their main form of defense. The Orcas would then engage in a "wound and withdraw" strategy, whereby adult Orcas, sometimes accompanied by calves, would attack in waves. If an individual Sperm Whale was successfully separated from the rosette, one or two other Sperm Whales would leave the rosette and flank the isolated individual in an act of protection, ultimately leading it back into the formation. Unfortunately, in this specific encounter, the Sperm Whales could not protect themselves sufficiently from the Orcas, leading to much bloodshed.

Off the southwestern tip of Australia, in Bremer Bay, an encounter between Sperm Whales and Orcas ended quite differently. While the Sperm Whales went into a marguerite formation, putting their calf in the middle for protection, the Orcas kept charging at them, only to be assaulted by a cloud of liquid Sperm Whale poo fondly known as a "poonado." In fact, the same Sperm Whale was seen to empty its bowels in quick succession in an effort to ward off the pesky Orcas that kept hounding them. Success was on the side of the Sperm Whales this time and the Orcas were left with no choice but to withdraw.

SHARK AND RAY ENCOUNTERS WITH ORCAS

While most encounters involve Orcas and marine mammals, some populations are known to feast on elasmobranchs—members of the shark and ray family. In New Zealand, off Mercury Island, Orcas appear to favor a very specific snack of stingrays when in the shallows. While this was considered the only population to feed on stingrays, more recent observations in the Sea of Cortez, off Mexico's Baja Peninsula, saw Orcas actively hunting mobulid rays, a skill passed on from mother to calf. Orcas of the KwaZulu-Natal region (northeast South Africa) and the Galápagos Islands were also seen trying to turn a giant manta ray upside down, ultimately breaching atop it in order to kill it. Manta rays are also taken as prey in the waters off Mayotte, in the Indian Ocean. Given that mobulid livers make up approximately 5 percent of their body mass, the liver can weigh as much as 20 lb (9 kg) in a sicklefin devil ray and 132 lb (60 kg) in an adult giant manta ray, which represents a significant source of energy to these Orcas.

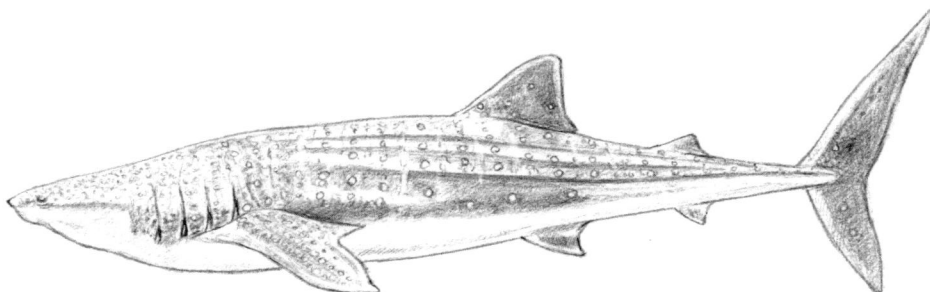

WHALE SHARK
These spotted giants are only whales by name but are, in fact, the largest fish on the planet.

In La Paz, Mexico, the members of the Moctezuma Orca pod work together to take down the largest fish on the planet, the whale shark. They start by ramming the slow-swimming plankton eater, which, in these waters is in its juvenile phase, to try and stun it. If it tries to "crash dive"—sink quickly to depths of as much as 5,900 ft (1,800 m)—the Orcas will bump and hit it to bring it back to the surface. Then, the Orcas work together to flip the beast onto its back to expose its vulnerable belly. (The skin on its back, some of the thickest of any animal, is too tough for predators' teeth to punch through.) Once the whale shark is flipped, they bite off its pelvic fins, leading it to bleed to death. The Orcas then feast on the fish's organs, including its fatty liver. This hunt attracts other species, like birds, which dive down into the chaos to grab their share. The Moctezuma pod appears to prefer cartilaginous fish, including stingrays, pygmy devil rays, and bull sharks.

Off the coast of South Africa, two male Orcas named for their rare and distinct collapsed dorsal fins using the nautical terms for left (Port) and right (Starboard) have made headlines by effortlessly preying on great white sharks, bronze whalers, and rare sevengill sharks (taking 17 in just one day in 2023). Dubbed "South Africa's shark slayers," the "deadly duo," and a series of other unflattering monikers, the pair have been documented taking down great white sharks, killing them and then ripping out the shark's enormous, fatty liver—the approximately 115-lb (52-kg) organ is so nutrient dense it completely fulfills the daily energy demands of an adult male Orca. Starboard was even spotted singlehandedly killing an over 8-ft (2.5-m) juvenile great white shark within two minutes, near South Africa's Mossel Bay. While Orcas are known to hunt cooperatively, Port, despite being seen hovering about 330 ft (100 m) away while the hunt took place, chose not to get involved.

This pair have successfully caused a mass displacement of great white sharks eastward, out of Gansbaai and Mossel Bay, an area that has depended on international tourists to dive with the great whites. As it turns out, cage-diving is species-agnostic, so tourists are still able to dive with sharks, but they are bronze whalers instead. Orcas continue to hunt these sharks in Mossel Bay, but unlike the great whites, their displacement is not permanent—they decrease in number for a week, after which their numbers rise again. "Bronzies" appear to be more akin to zebras that return to the same area despite predation from lions, while great white sharks cannot seem to cope with this level of predation. While we thought this hunt of great white sharks by Orcas was limited to South Africa, more recently, a shark carcass washed up near Cape Bridgewater, Victoria, Australia, and DNA analysis confirmed Orca predation, marking the first confirmed instance of Orcas preying on great white sharks in Australian waters.

Humpback feeding

Orcas are not the only species that build a net out of bubbles to trap their prey. One or more Humpbacks (*Megaptera novaeangliae*) will come together and blow a continuous ring of bubbles from their blowholes while encircling or corralling a school of krill or fish. The bubbles rise, creating a curtain or net that confines prey. The whales then accelerate and swim through the bubble-net with their mouths agape, engulfing the prey-laden water. Humpbacks are some of the only baleen whales that are seen to feed cooperatively.

Lunge-feeding rorquals

Fin Whales (*Balaenoptera physalus*), like other rorquals (but not all baleen whales!) are often seen lunge feeding among other members of their species. They

LUNGE FEEDING
A Fin Whale lunge feeds in an effort to fulfill its energetic needs.

accelerate with their mouths agape at 90 degrees through dense prey patches. On each lunge, the whales expand their rubbery throat pleats up to four times their resting size. This is only possible because the two halves of their lower jaw are connected to their skull by flexible joints, and their tips aren't fused together, allowing them to swing outward and widen their mouth. Their tongue flattens against the bottom of their mouth, also creating more space.

Each gulp accommodates about 22 lb (10 kg) of krill swarming in about 18,500 gallons (70,000 l) of water. For a Fin Whale that weighs nearly 50 tons (45,000 kg), this volume of water exceeds the weight of the feeding animal, giving the whale a bloated tadpole shape rather than its usual streamlined body. However, in no time at all, once the whales close their mouths, the pleats contract. The tongue returns to its normal shape, pushing against the water. The engulfed water is filtered out of the distended throat pouch as it gradually deflates, and the whale swallows the prey stuck to its baleen plates. One feeding lunge is insufficient to provide a Fin Whale's daily calorie needs, and so it repeats these actions over several hours, within which time it will ingest more than a ton of krill—enough for it to get on with its daily chores.

Blue Whales, being larger, can use this method to swallow half a million calories in one gulp, which is about the equivalent of eating 2,000 burgers a day. With each lunge, they fill their mouths up so much, they could fit an adult Humpback inside! Luckily for the Humpback, Blue Whales could not swallow them however —their throats are so small, they would choke on a loaf of bread.

I have had the privilege to witness a large group of lunge-feeding Humpback Whales in the waters off Monterey Bay, California, in a particularly productive year. The whales' heads emerge powerfully out of the water with their mouths open and barnacle-encrusted throat pleats distended, ensuring they can take in as large a mouthful of prey-laden water as possible. From the corners of their mouths, fish attempt to escape from the literal jaws of death. The whale then closes its mouth and forces the water out through its baleen plates to ensure it gets its desired and very much required calories. This visually striking scene often leaves watchers in awe.

Benthic or bottom suction feeders

Not all baleen whales lunge feed, and not all favor fish for lunch. Gray Whales prefer benthic invertebrates like shrimp and worms buried in the sediment at the bottom of the ocean. To feed, they roll on their sides (most Gray Whales favor the right side) and bring their mouths as close as possible to the sediment. They then swim along the bottom and suction up (by depressing their tongue) the sediment and prey. The sediment and water are filtered out of the baleen. While not the most visible feeding display, the whale streams sediment from its mouth and stirs up plumes of mud in the process, leaving tell-tale tracks behind it. In general, when baleen whales feed, their impact on the environment is minimal because they simply extract fish. In the case of Gray Whales, however, they leave behind excavated pits that range in size from 22 to 215 sq ft (2–20 m²), creating between 2,700 and 3,200 pits in one feeding season.

Within seconds of creating these pits, scavenging invertebrates arrive en masse, up to 30 times more than in the undisturbed areas. The move is initiated by scavenging lysianassid amphipods, small (less than ½ in/10 mm) crustaceans that eat dead, organic material. These amphipods make the most of the crustaceans and polychaete worms injured during the whale feeding event. Within hours, this amphipod species moves on and is replaced by different genera of scavenging lysianassid amphipods. Over weeks, the organic material trapped in these pits attracts other colonists.

During excavation, Gray Whales also re-suspend sediment and nutrients on the seafloor, an action that enhances productivity. Ghost shrimp that rarely emerge from their burrows rear their heads and become available to anything that fancies them. Seabirds, particularly surf scoters or sea ducks, do not pass up this opportunity, especially in spring when food is in low supply, and they are

GRAY WHALE FEEDING
Gray Whales seek out benthic invertebrates like shrimp and worms buried in the sediment.

preparing for reproduction and migration. In this way, Gray Whale benthic feeding does much more than fill their bellies, providing ample opportunities for a range of other species to also indulge in a feast.

Energy-efficient feeding

In the upper Gulf of Thailand in Southeast Asia, Bryde's Whales (*Balaenoptera edeni*) use energy-efficient feeding methods in shallow waters. This area is known to be hypoxic (low in oxygen), because of the eutrophication (excessive richness of nutrients) released by the outflow of sewage from several large rivers. This makes most of the water body uninhabitable for many species except at the water surface, where fish like anchovies thrive. To make the most of these abundant surface schools of fish, the Bryde's Whales lift their heads above the water with their mouths closed. They then tread water open-mouthed, their lower jaws making contact with the sea surface. This helps create a current of

A BRYDE'S WHALE FEEDING AT THE SURFACE
Some whales feed at the depths of the ocean, while others do the very opposite.

water straight into their mouths. Throughout, the whales continuously and gently move their flippers and tails to maintain their position and stability in the water, waiting patiently for fish to enter. Once the fish swim in, the whales close their mouths and engulf the prey underwater.

The limited movements used in this behavior make it more energy efficient than lunge feeding. Given its specificity to this group, this behavior appears to be socially learned, since scientists have documented mothers and calves tread-water feeding in the area as well.

Easy pickings: The sardine run

The KwaZulu-Natal sardine run of southern Africa is one of the greatest wildlife spectacles on the planet. Between May and July, billions of sardines—particularly the Southern African pilchard—spawn in the cool temperate waters off the Agulhas Bank on the southernmost tip of the continent, traveling northward along the east coast of South Africa into the subtropical waters of the Indian Ocean. This movement is triggered by these 10-in (25-cm) sardines from the Atlantic Ocean straying too far into southern waters and experiencing a brief pulse of cold upwelling along the coast. These cold-adapted fish then follow the chilly currents northeast until they reach the warm waters of the Indian Ocean. Here, the upwelling ends, leaving them stranded in a challenging subtropical habitat.

This journey through increasingly inhospitable conditions, from familiar to unfamiliar seas, is not an easy one. The sardine shoals extend as long as 9 miles (15 km), as wide as 2 miles (3.5 km) and can run as deep as 130 ft (40 m)—needless to say, these billions of sardines do not travel alone, because where there is food, there are predators. Cetaceans are the first to arrive—super pods of Common Dolphins (*Delphinus delphis*) and Pantropical Spotted Dolphins (*Stenella attenuata*) tightly round up the sardines into "bait balls" the size of squash courts, which they then rip through, snatching fish after fish. They are soon followed by a crew of sharks—bronze whalers, duskies, gray nurse sharks, blacktips, spinners, and zambezis—which snap at the fish in the hopes of getting a mouthful here and there. Large game fish like mackerel and tuna also want to partake in the buffet and are accompanied by penguins, Cape fur seals and dive-bombing Cape gannets that leave behind cavitation trails (streams of bubbles created when an animal moves rapidly through the water). The gannets number in their hundreds and rain down into the surface waters like missiles. Last but not least, with mouths agape and throat pleats stretched, the Humpback, Bryde's, and Minke Whales make their grand entrance to avoid being left out. While the Humpback Whales lunge feed, the Bryde's Whales engulf entire bait balls of sardines amidst the frenzy. Despite the huge numbers of fish, the sardine run involves only a fraction (less than 10 percent) of South Africa's Southern African pilchard population.

Dolphins that hunt with tools

We often think of tool use as the domain of humans, chimpanzees, and crows. However, dolphins have also been known to engage in tool use, which should not come as a surprise, since dolphins rank among the smartest animals on Earth.

SPONGES AND SHELL TOOLS

In Shark Bay, Western Australia, a select group of Bottlenose Dolphins have developed a technique called "sponging," which involves picking up a piece of fresh basket sponge off the seafloor and wrapping it around their rostrum before digging around on the sandy bottoms of underwater channels in search of their favorite bottom-dwelling fish like sandperches, gobies, and flatfish. As these fish lack swim bladders, they become invisible to echolocating dolphins and would be overlooked as a source of food, but sponging dolphins can find them by digging around. This means they are able to exploit a different food source than their non-sponging counterparts. The sponge also provides protection from sharp rocks, stingrays, urchins, and other hazards. Once a fish is disturbed, the dolphins drop the sponge and grab the fish. Sponging is a culturally transmitted behavior. Discovered by scientists as recently as 1997, this behavior dates back about 180 years to a single female nicknamed "Sponging Eve." This time-consuming tradition is vertically transmitted from mothers to daughters, indicating a strong female bias. Around 91 percent of female calves adopt sponging from their sponging mothers, while only 50 percent of males do.

While spongers tend to be seen alone, they are known to show social homophily, which is the tendency of individuals to associate and bond with similar others, as in the proverb "birds of a feather flock together," with both male and female spongers more likely to spend time with other spongers. Both genders also tend to forage more and rest less than their non-sponging counterparts. Sponging is an energetically costly behavior, as the foraging grounds are often a few feet deeper than the sand flats where other, non-sponging dolphins hunt. Despite this, spongers do not seem to experience reduced reproductive success.

Sponges are not the only tools used by dolphins in Shark Bay. They have also been documented using shells to collect lunch! The dolphin traps underwater prey in a large sea snail shell, pokes its beak into the opening, lifts the shell above the surface of the water and shakes it until all the contents end up in its mouth, much like one of us trying to get the last crumbs out of a chip packet. This behavior appears rare, with only 42 shelling events by 19 individuals observed over 11

SPONGING
This ingenious technique is practiced exclusively by Bottlenose Dolphins living in Shark Bay, Australia.

years in the mid-1990s that included over 5,000 dolphin group encounters. However, other encounters may be missed because the behavior occurs in bouts of a few seconds. Unlike sponging behavior, this is not a vertically transmitted behavior but is instead horizontally passed on from peer to peer.

SPINNING TO FEED DEEP

In the Azores islands in the mid-Atlantic, Risso's Dolphins (*Grampus griseus*), despite being mostly nocturnal shallow-water foragers, can dive to depths of 165–2,000 ft (50–600 m) in search of fish and their favored prey, cephalopods. Their target dive is actively chosen and pre-planned, based on the information they've previously gathered about the depths at which to find their prey. Why not target the deep-scattering layer when you know it contains high densities and varieties of tasty fish and cephalopods that suit your taste?

To get to these depths, they have to use a very particular dive strategy to optimize their prey capture efficiency. First, the dolphin exhales to reduce buoyancy. It then begins to fluke powerfully, then rotates to the right side, all within the first second of the dive. Once it achieves negative buoyancy, the dolphin glides downward, fast, while rotating slowly. Named a "spin dive," this exclusive foraging dive is faster and angled more steeply downward than a non-spin dive, allowing the dolphin to dive deeper (twice as deep, in fact, than a non-spin dive) and reach its prey faster. Interestingly, all spin dives are right-sided, indicating that lateralization, where a behavior is more dominantly performed on one side than the other, exists in this species. When diving and foraging at shallower depths, the dolphins used non-spin dives, which are less energetically demanding. But the fact that they do choose to use spin dives, for deep dives that cost much more in terms of energy, indicates their confidence in the bounty of food that will provide good return on their investment.

When hunting skills aren't enough

Even the best hunters, the apex predators, sometimes struggle to find food because of things beyond their control—like shifts in the environment. Southern resident Killer Whale (SRKW, which we would prefer to call SR Orca) pods in the Salish Sea, Puget Sound, and other areas of the Pacific Northwest have a penchant for Chinook salmon, which makes up 80–90 percent of their diet. It is the largest and fattiest of all Pacific salmon, and is chosen over any other fish species because it provides the biggest calorie intake per fish. However, as Chinook salmon populations are threatened with extinction due to over-fishing, the construction of dams that interfere with their ability to spawn, and warming waters due to climate change, they are getting progressively thinner and declining in numbers. This leaves SRKWs struggling to find sufficient food, which results in miscarriages and the death of newborns. Worryingly, post-reproductive (menopausal) matriarchs, who are a key source of knowledge and teaching for younger generations, are also dying.

While Orcas are known to supplement their diets with other fish like chum salmon, coho salmon, steelhead trout, and non-salmonid species like lingcod and Pacific halibut, Chinook salmon has long been linked to their survivability. The Chinook salmon shortage is cited as one of the primary causes for the decline of the SRKW population, which now stands at approximately 73 individuals. Sadly, the population size has remained relatively static for the past 50 years, with an initial decline in population size at the beginning of the twentieth century due to their slaughter for meat and blubber and the capture of SRKWs en masse for use in aquariums. The population only received respite when Canada banned their capture in the 1970s. However, it seems like this period was the straw that broke the camel's back, and today, the decline in older, fatter, bigger Chinook has added to the challenges faced by this population. The survival and protection of Chinook salmon is therefore vital to this Orca population's survival.

Strangely, northern resident Orcas that feed on similar prey species have been increasing in number over the last 40 years, with a current population size of about 300 individuals. This stark difference in population numbers between the northern and southern residents, two populations that overlap significantly in their territory and have similar social structures and reproductive behavior, might be down to how the two populations hunt for salmon, their primary and preferred food source. While both populations use echolocation to hunt their prey, females are the predominant hunters within the northern resident population, while the opposite is true for the southern resident population. If the mother was alive, the northern resident males hunted less, which is expected, but in the southern resident population, males captured more prey and spent more time foraging compared to the females. The only commonality is that females hunted less when accompanied by a calf, which is understandable, since there is likely some risk to leaving the calf temporarily with a babysitter while hunting, or because of the time demands of nursing a calf. This was particularly so with the southern residents where females with calves never caught prey.

Curiously, when in the Salish Sea in summer and fall, SRKWs have an abundance of Chinook salmon available to them compared to their healthier northern relatives. However, their populations still lag behind those of their cousins. The big question is, what happens when the SRKWs are outside the Salish Sea? Do they have abundant prey during the winter and spring months? Perhaps their food source is less abundant during this time. That said, better

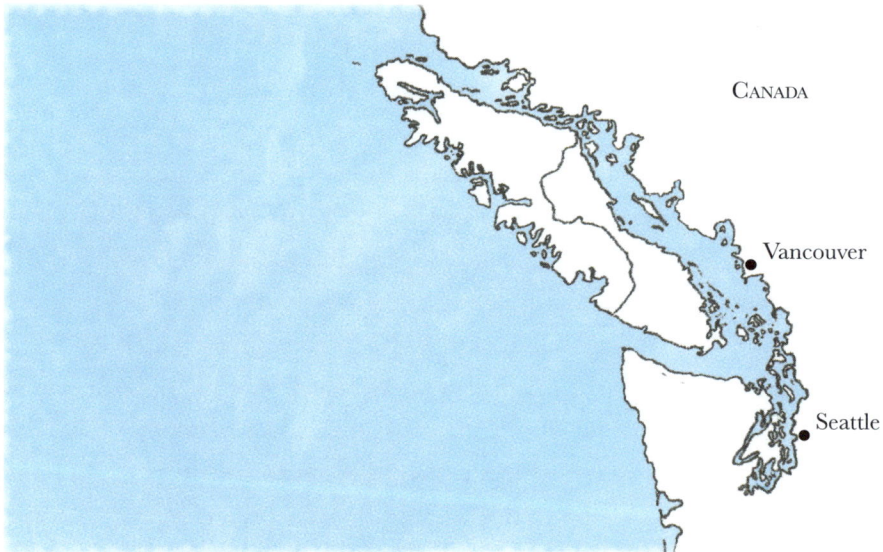

THE SALISH SEA
This region is an important habitat and source of abundant food for SRKWs.

availability while in the Salish Sea does not immediately indicate they can access this food source. SRKWs also encounter more ships in the Salish Sea during this period of Chinook abundance. The noise from ships masks their communication and interferes with their ability to hunt to success.

The difference could be that southern resident Orcas are evolving as they try to feed themselves. The females in this population are more vulnerable to disturbances from vessel noise, which may relate to their less successful hunts compared to the males in their population. Reducing these disturbances will be important to ensuring the population succeeds in the long term. As such, commercial shipping in Washington state has been asked to voluntarily reduce speed to reduce cavitation from their propellors and the resulting noise. So, abundance of prey alone does not determine whether SRKWs will thrive in the future, because it is clearly more complicated than that.

DIGESTION

Digestion varies between different species of whale. To take one example, in Sperm Whales, food goes from the mouth to the esophagus and then slips into the first stomach chamber, where it is stored for digestion. Food is broken down mechanically in the forestomach through muscular contractions and in the main stomach, where the food undergoes acid breakdown. The grand finale is the pyloric chamber, which is responsible for further breaking down food and neutralizing stomach acid before it passes into the small intestine. Most nutrient absorption occurs in the intestine. Sperm whales have a longer small-intestine-to-body-size ratio than Humpback Whales, which is typical of baleen whales.

Sperm Whales have four stomachs, while Spade-toothed Beaked Whales (*Mesoplodon traversii*) and Baird's Beaked Whales (*Berardius bairdii*) have as many as thirteen! Multiple stomachs mean these whales can swallow large quantities of food without chewing, and once in, food is digested and nutrients extracted.

While Sperm Whales have shown that they like being different in many ways, from the shape of their heads to the placement of their blowholes, there is something else that sets them apart from their cousins: ambergris. This is the solid, waxy substance produced in the digestive systems of Sperm Whales which enables them to feast on their favorite food—squid (for more on ambergris, see Chapter 9). Eventually ambergris is excreted as a smelly, dung-like substance. Once exposed to sunlight and salt water, it dries up, solidifies, and develops a musky smell. In other species, such as Blue Whales, feces reflect the color of the food they feast on. And so in Sri Lankan waters, where Blue Whales feed on bright red sergestid shrimp, their poo is, accordingly, bright red. This shows that feces is not a mere byproduct, but something that can be beautiful and that tells many stories.

7

MIGRATION AND MOVEMENT

There are 4,508 migratory species on our planet, of which about a quarter are endangered. These species roam our oceans and land in search of food that will allow them to thrive and seek mates to ensure their genes and kind might persist. Animals traverse country borders without knowledge of their existence and in the ocean they can travel even further, unhindered, in search of what they need. Some migrate vertically through the water column, others horizontally across ocean basins, but all are simply seeking favorable conditions and a chance to survive.

CETACEAN MIGRATION

Marine mammals are well known for their annual, wide-ranging migrations between feeding and breeding grounds. They invest heavily in the success of this journey by first feeding heartily and then investing in the next generation as if their lives depended on it—which they do. Because they often traverse through the backyards of multiple countries and even continents, their protection hinges on collective goodwill, with these countries coming together to recognize their individual responsibility to protect these species, for our common heritage. The Convention on the Conservation of Migratory Species of Wild Animals, commonly known as CMS, is a global treaty ensuring that responsibility is placed on every country a species might journey through as well as any areas beyond national jurisdiction. Appendix I, which lists species threatened with extinction, currently lists 15 cetacean species, while Appendix II lists 43 species and includes those that need or would significantly benefit from international cooperation.

The success of these efforts requires an understanding of the needs of these species, the protection of important habitats, and a little self-reflection.

Why do whales migrate?
Across our oceans, cold, nutrient-rich water from the depths moves upward to the surface continuously through upwelling. At the poles, this water can support

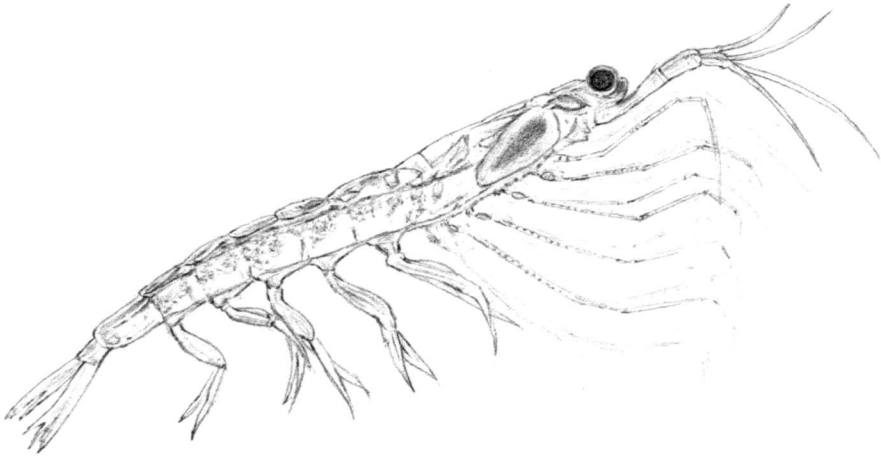

ANTARCTIC KRILL
Phytoplankton and krill abound in nutrient-packed polar waters.

the growth of an abundance of phytoplankton (microscopic marine algae), which subsequently gives rise to an enormous amount of krill (small crustaceans that are part of a diverse group of invertebrates that includes crabs, lobsters, shrimp, copepods, amphipods, and more sessile creatures like barnacles). Baleen whales love to feast on krill, with some eating up to 4.4 tons (4 tonnes) daily (about the same weight as an adult elephant), flocking to the poles annually to fill up before migrating to their breeding grounds. They begin their journeys to warmer waters and familiar breeding grounds as their higher-latitude polar feeding grounds begin to cool, decreasing day length and light shuts productivity down, and ice forms, making it difficult for them to remain. Baleen whales return to the same breeding and feeding grounds, year after year after year—some scientists even believe that this strong preference plays a role in the decline in numbers of North Atlantic Right Whales (*Eubalaena glacialis*). Despite their habitat being cut through by extremely busy shipping lanes, North Atlantic Right Whales keep returning. While at first it may not seem to make sense to return to a dangerous place, it does if this is where all the food is.

Recently, many (humans, not whales) have pondered the question, "Why move?" As many whale species are large, remaining in their high-latitude, cold, productive feeding grounds to give birth would avoid the costs of migration, particularly as some species do not feed while on their migratory routes.

However, many theories exist as to why they opt to migrate. Some speculate that the mothers migrate to find warmer areas in which to give birth, because warm waters mean calves can put more energy into growth and survival rather than wasting energy in keeping warm, given that their blubber reserves are not at full thickness yet. While this might be a driver, the presence of newborn Orca (*Orcinus orca*) calves in the frigid waters of Antarctica suggests otherwise. Another train of thought posits that it reduces predation events on calves because there are fewer Orcas around to mount attacks, as Orcas favor high latitudes where seals are commonly found. This makes sense if you consider whales a "fight" or "flight" species.

Flight species, such as Blue (*Balaenoptera musculus*), Sei (*B. borealis*), Minke (*B. acutorostrata*), and Fin (*B. physalus*) whales, swim away as fast as possible when approached by Orcas. They are some of the fastest whales in our oceans, their speed facilitated by their streamlined bodies and skin, so catching up to them requires a prolonged chase, which may not make energetic sense to a hungry

SEI WHALE
*The Sei Whale is one of the fastest whales of all, reaching
speeds of close to 30 miles per hour in short bursts.*

predator. They also tend to calve in open water, so cornering them is a bit tricky, and perhaps this wide and unpredictable dispersal means it is too much of an investment for Orcas to even look for them in the vast ocean.

Fight species, on the other hand, are slow-moving whales that tend to stand their ground and put up a fight if approached by the Orcas, if only because they cannot move fast enough to get away. They calve in shallow coastal waters or lagoons, which makes defense easy—particularly when the Orcas are trying to drown the calves—they use coastal migratory corridors, and they often have hardened patches of skin or barnacle encrustations that can amount to as much as ½ ton (450 kg) in weight! This may sound incredibly heavy, but for a whale that weighs almost 80 times this, it is akin to simply donning another layer of clothing.

Skin regenerating theory

A third and more recent theory suggests that migration to warm waters allows whales to maintain healthy skin. Warm waters increase skin metabolism and hasten skin molts in an environment that does not sap the heat out of their body. Large whales in cold waters typically host a film of yellow diatoms (microscopic unicellular photosynthetic algae that produce intricate, glassy cell walls composed of silica and are ubiquitous in the ocean) on their skin because they are busy trying to conserve body heat by diverting blood flow away from the surface of their skin. Less blood flow at the surface means reduced skin regeneration, which, in turn, prevents skin sloughing or molting.

However, when in warm water, loss of body heat is not life-threatening, and blood instead flows to the skin surface to keep the whales cool. This also results in them molting, ridding themselves of these diatoms, and making way for healthier skin. Therefore, skin sloughing is a "self-cleaning" method for these whales. In the past, whalers would identify whales that had just migrated from the tropics by their clean skin compared to those that remained in polar waters with yellowing skin. They even called Blue Whales in polar waters "sulfur bottom whales" because of the yellow film forming on their underbellies.

While we do not fully understand the drivers for whale migrations, and maybe we never will, we can assume there is good reason for completely uprooting and heading out into the somewhat unknown, coming head to head with potential predators and shifting environmental conditions. Even less is known about when, in their evolutionary history, whales began these costly long-range movements. One hypothesis suggests that migrations began about 3 MYA, when massive ice sheets started spreading across the Northern Hemisphere, preventing whales from remaining in their favorite habitats and constraining where their favorite foods could flourish, forcing them on long journeys to seek shelter and meals.

The greatest migrations and their challenges

Gray Whales (*Eschrichtius robustus*) have the longest migration of any mammal in the world. They outdo the longest migrating terrestrial mammal by thousands of miles. Gray Whales typically spend their summers in the chilly waters of the northern Pacific and their winters along the coasts of California and Mexico, which amounts to a return trip of about 10,000 miles (16,000 km). However, in 2013, one male 40-ft (12-m) Gray Whale traveled from a small population in the western Pacific to Walvis Bay in Namibia, where he spent a few months. While it is unclear whether this potentially 16,700-mile (26,800-km) trip was made on purpose or by accident, it is possible that the rapidly melting Arctic sea ice opened up new pathways around Canada before the whale then proceeded across the Atlantic and south along Africa's west coast.

The longest great-circle distance (the shortest distance between two points along a sphere) was traveled by a male Humpback Whale (*Megaptera novaeangliae*) that crossed two oceans and two breeding grounds many thousands of miles apart. The distance between when it was first sighted on the Pacific coast of Colombia and then in Zanzibar in the southwest Indian Ocean, where it was spotted in 2022, is estimated to be 8,106 miles (13,046 km) at minimum, with no way for us ever to find out how much more it might have traveled on its nine-year journey. This happy coincidence was discovered through photo-identification images taken by citizen scientists over the years. We will never know whether the whale made this epic journey because of food stock depletion due to rising sea temperatures or to find a mate. Regard-

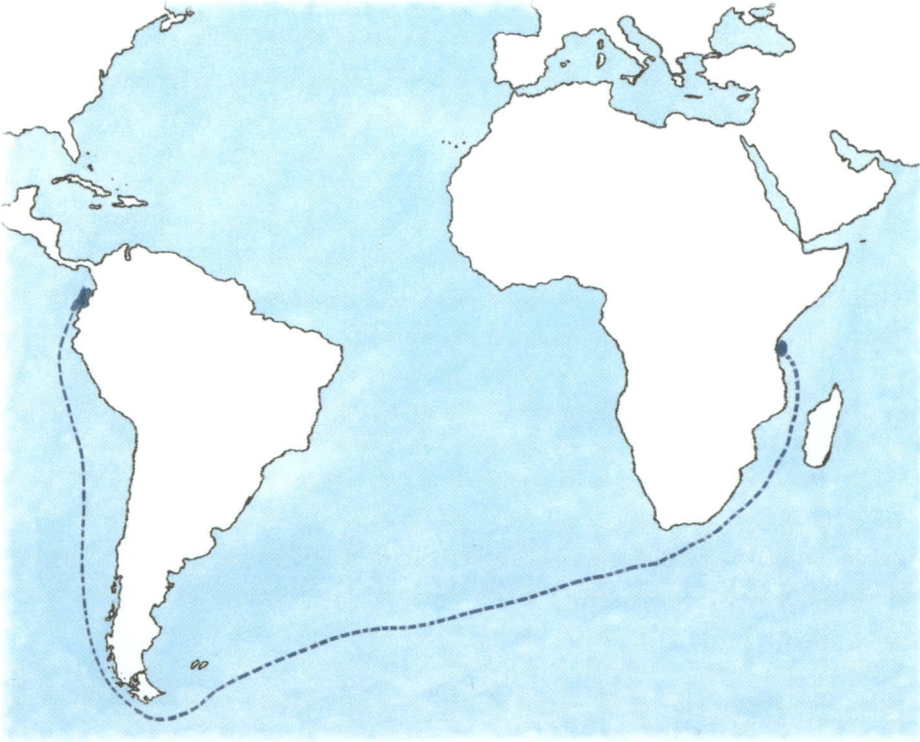

IMPRESSIVE JOURNEYS
One male Humpback Whale is known to have traveled from the Pacific
coast of Colombia to Zanzibar in the Indian Ocean.

less, this record-breaking feat is something to marvel at.

These great migrations take place so flawlessly, with whales returning annually to specific feeding locations, that researchers have been seeking answers to how they do it for many years. Recently, they coupled historical whaling data from American and Soviet whaling logbooks dating back over 200 years with modern satellite tracking data of six large whale species (amounting to 1,155 deployed tags). Incredibly, they found that whales integrate magnetic and astronomic orientation cues to find their way between their feeding, breeding, and calving areas.

Long-distance migrations are, unsurprisingly, vulnerable to climate change. Rising sea temperatures may shift prey distribution, causing whales to shift off their previous migration route, which could lead to new and unknown challenges. For the whales, shifting is just one option; the others include dying or adapting—which is hard if temperature increases occur faster than normal. In fact, with Humpback Whales, it is estimated that as sea temperatures rise, almost 37–67 percent (depending on the extent of our continued use of fossil fuels) of existing breeding areas will become too warm, with temperatures surpassing the whales' preferred 70–82°F (21–28°C) range. While some might shift to northern breeding sites, those that rely on the isolated breeding ground of Hawaii, for example, will be left high and dry.

Feeding areas might also be at risk. For baleen whales that depend on swarming species like krill, a decline in prey populations can have serious domino effects on the whales themselves. In preparation for migration, Humpback Whales gorge on krill in Antarctic waters. However, an 80 percent decline in krill populations since the 1970s due to reduced sea ice because of warming temperatures means less food for the whales and potentially more overlap between fishers and whales vying for these limited resources in intersecting areas. The risk of entanglement will increase, as will the risk of noise pollution and collisions with vessels.

The physiology of migrating whales

For capital breeders like female Humpback Whales, which do not feed throughout their migration but instead use their stored energy accumulated in their feeding grounds, the toll of migration is not insignificant. An average-sized Humpback Whale mother, 42 ft (12.7 m) long and weighing in at nearly 39 tons (35 tonnes), will lose approximately 12 tons (11 tonnes) of blubber tissue. This is the equivalent of consuming 63 tons (57 tonnes) of krill during her migration.

For Western Australian Humpback Whales migrating north from their feeding to breeding grounds, body condition, which is the amount of stored energy an individual has, or the organism's health, which is a reflection of past feeding success, decreased by 23 percent for juveniles and 13 percent for adults. East Australian Humpbacks have also shown a decrease in body condition during their migration between feeding and breeding grounds, with juveniles losing 18 percent and adults losing 10 percent of their body condition. North Atlantic Right

THE WESTERN AUSTRALIAN HUMPBACK WHALE
These wonderful creatures are making a comeback and are frequently seen breaching.

Whale juveniles also had higher daily energetic needs than adults. As with all children, regardless of species, smaller individuals, such as juvenile whales, experience a higher loss of body condition because they have a higher mass-specific metabolic rate (the amount of energy used per unit of body mass over a given period). This higher rate means they require more energy per pound of body weight to do anything, leading to increased energy consumption.

Fatter animals, or those with higher energy reserves, can fast longer during migration and breeding periods. For females, extra energy means they can invest better in their growing offspring and ensure their survival. Among the Western Australian Humpback populations, the yearlings migrate north to the breeding grounds first. These juveniles have just been weaned after a year of feasting on their mother's nutrient-rich milk, which fattens them sufficiently for a successful journey. The adult males are next to leave, followed by the resting females and, finally, the pregnant females. This is unsurprising given that the latter group must maximize their time spent on the feeding grounds to ensure success on the breeding grounds.

The longer the female is, the longer the calf is, whether it is the Western Australian, Eastern Australian, Eastern South Pacific Humpbacks, the Northern or Southern Right Whales, or the Eastern North Pacific Gray Whales. So while the calf's body condition initially correlates with the mother's, as the breeding season proceeds, this correlation turns negative, with the mother's body condition declining while the calf's body condition improves. This is as expected, given that the mother is investing everything she possibly can of her finite energy stores in her newborn calf, which she must ensure is of an appropriate size and muscle mass for the upcoming journey. Being big and strong ensures good swimming ability, comfortable breathing on surfacing, and survival. Southern Right and Gray Whale mothers are said to lose 23–25 percent of their body condition during this phase, with maternal loss being proportional to investment in the calf.

Eastern South Pacific Humpback Whales travel on a nearly 10,000-mile (16,000-km) round trip from the coastal waters of Ecuador, Colombia, and Costa Rica to the Western Antarctic Peninsula (WAP). When they reach their feeding grounds in the WAP, they focus on feeding on the abundance of Antarctic krill in preparation for their next migration. During this time, all whales show an improvement in body condition as they indulge. When they first arrive at the WAP, they feed rapidly. Over time, their feeding rate decreases, with feeding bouts mostly happening at night. Despite the reduced feeding rate, their mass continues to increase, as seen in North Atlantic Fin, Sei, and Minke whales. As it turns out, in places like the Weddell Sea, the total fat content of krill continues to increase through the feeding season, while the amount of krill increases in inshore waters. So, while they feed less, the better-quality krill in nearshore waters likely allows them to keep stocking up on their energy reserves through this period.

Lactating females also improve their body condition through the feeding season. Still, no matter how much they feast, their body condition lags behind that of mature males and non-pregnant females. Lactation is the most energetically demanding phase in the reproductive cycle, so it is no surprise. Eastern

South Pacific lactating female Humpbacks are not the only ones that struggle to catch up, since this has also been seen amongst the Pacific Coast feeding group of Gray Whales, North Atlantic Humpbacks, Sei, and Fin whales. The most rapid increases in body condition are seen amongst the calves and juveniles, which invest the energy gained in skeletal growth during the breeding season, unlike the adults, which invest it in reproduction.

EASTERN SOUTH PACIFIC HUMPBACK WHALES
These incredible travelers make a regular 10,000-mile round-trip migration between the Western Antarctic Peninsula and the coastal waters of Ecuador, Colombia, and Costa Rica.

Non-migratory whales

Not all large whales migrate. Some species of Bryde's Whales (*Balaenoptera edeni*), all Bowhead Whales (*Balaena mysticetus*), and even the world's smallest baleen whale, the Pygmy Right Whale (*Caperea marginata*), do not migrate anywhere in their range. The northern Indian Ocean is home to two non-migratory whale populations known to migrate in other parts of their range: the Northern Indian Ocean Pygmy Blue Whale (*Balaenoptera musculus indica*) and the Arabian Sea Humpback Whale.

The Northern Indian Ocean Pygmy Blue Whale has a limited range that ensures these whales remain in the warm waters of the northern Indian Ocean throughout their lives. I owe my career to these whales, because it was as an intern at the start of my journey that I discovered they were non-migratory in nature. I spotted an aggregation of Blue Whales on the island's south coast and assumed, as I was taught as an undergraduate, that they would be breeding and calving. Satisfied with this hope, I requested that our research vessel deviate off course to voyeuristically watch six whales tightly packed in an area the size of a soccer field. Of course, on arrival, I quickly realized that there was no breeding (zero penises in sight) nor calving (no babies!) but having convinced the captain to come this far, I requested a few extra minutes of observation before we continued on our way.

PYGMY RIGHT WHALE
The smallest of all baleen whales.

Luckily, the whales did not disappoint—one of them released a bright red substance that I soon realized was its feces. While not many people would have been excited at this sight, this was my eureka moment. The fact that the whales were pooing meant they were feeding in the area—which was unexpected because textbooks and professors told us they fed in cold, polar regions where oceans were productive enough to support these giants. Regardless, this moment hooked me, and I knew immediately that the Blue Whales in Sri Lankan waters were doing something remarkably different from what we thought they should do. I started calling them "the unorthodox whales." In time, my work as a result of this encounter shifted what we knew or thought we knew about Blue Whales and highlighted the importance of tropical ecosystems to the lives of the largest animal that has ever roamed our planet.

Apart from feeding, they also do as they are expected to in warm waters. They breed, as evidenced by the ménage-à-trois behaviors often seen, where two males will chase down a female at high speeds in a bid to mate with her; eventually one ends up the victor and the other swims away. They also calve, as evidenced by the presence of very young, tiny calves (~20 ft/~6 m) and a solitary record of a pregnant female that became stranded and gave birth in the Trincomalee Harbor on the east coast of Sri Lanka (the core of their range) on January 23, 1946. While these whales are truly the giants of the oceans, they enjoy keeping their private lives private, making this one of only two records of a Blue Whale birth anywhere on the planet.

Why do they remain in these warm waters that are less productive than cooler ones? As it turns out, these homebodies have a unique palate. They feed primarily on sergestid shrimp rather than krill (the top food choice of Blue Whales in other ocean basins), which are present abundantly in the northern Indian Ocean within a depth of 985 ft (300 m). Since the whales have to dive deeper to catch these shrimp, Northern Indian Ocean Blue Whales are often seen lifting their flukes before a deep dive, a behavior they do more often than other populations worldwide, to torpedo themselves downward. I also suspect that while most whales are gorgers, traveling to cold waters and feasting to their hearts' content, the Blue Whales in these warm waters are grazers, feeding on smaller quantities but often.

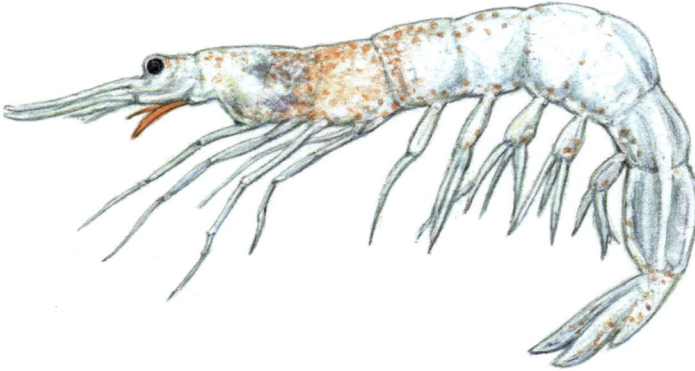

SERGESTID SHRIMP
Sergestid shrimp are the preferred prey of Blue Whales in the northern Indian Ocean with some being bioluminescent and producing light using photophores along their bodies.

The Arabian Sea Humpback Whale, which resides within the tropical Arabian Sea along the coast of Oman, is also known to refrain from seasonal migrations between high-latitude feeding grounds and low-latitude areas. These whales remain near Oman for the most part, occasionally traversing the Arabian Sea to the west coast of India. Apart from their songs, this population differs from the Humpback Whale populations of the Southern Hemisphere based on when they breed. The breeding cycle of the Arabian Sea Humpback Whale is the same as that of Humpback Whale populations that have made their home in the Northern Hemisphere (like the North Pacific or North Atlantic Humpback Whales), which extends from December to March. On the other hand, the breeding season of the whales in the Southern Hemisphere extends from July to October. Perhaps this lack of synchronicity in somewhat adjacent populations has evolved to prevent any chance of inbreeding.

A unique climate and abundance

What is so special about the northern Indian Ocean that not just one but two different baleen whale species have made it their permanent home? Well, home is where the food is. Migrating south to Antarctica from the central part of the northern Indian Ocean does not make sense energetically, and going north is not an option because the Eurasian landmass caps the Indian Ocean. So why migrate when you don't have to—particularly when your home is sufficiently productive? Food is in sufficient supply throughout the year thanks to the unique monsoon circulation and how it interacts with the seafloor and surroundings, ensuring that the whales meet their needs throughout the year.

The ability of these whales to feed year-round in the area depends on the intricate oceanographic dynamics of this part of the ocean basin. Of major cause for concern are changes in oceanographic conditions due to climate change, which may lead to shifts in the amount and locations of prey available for feeding. With rapidly warming oceans, the temperature of the Indian Ocean has been rising consistently and faster than all other ocean basins, bar the Arctic. Warmer conditions may reduce the abundance and primary productivity of phytoplankton, the base of all marine food webs—which can, in

THE ARABIAN SEA HUMPBACK WHALE
The uniquely patterned flukes of a young Humpback in the tropical Arabian Sea.

turn, have knock-on impacts on species higher up the food chain. In the northern Indian Ocean, the Arabian Sea Humpback Whale population is listed as Endangered, while the Northern Indian Ocean Pygmy Blue Whale population is listed as Data Deficient on the IUCN Red List of Threatened Species—both face a plethora of threats; many of which are human-caused. Despite being such enigmatic animals, we know very little about the whales in this area. Understanding them better is essential to designing the best course of action for their long-term protection.

Population shifts and returns

In the early 1980s in the Galápagos, two vocal clans of Sperm Whales (*Physeter macrocephalus*) roamed freely. Known as the "regular" and "+1" clans, as we saw in Chapter 5, they comprised many hundreds of individuals grouped by their coda preferences (the patterned series of clicks used by sperm whales for communication). The area provided all they needed until suddenly, after 14 years, their numbers started to decline. By the early 2000s, there were no longer Sperm Whales in these waters. This decline indicated a shift, potentially eastward, to coastal waters that were perhaps more favorable.

What happened next, however, surprised researchers who had dedicated themselves to tracking the clans in these waters. In 2013 and 2014, they began documenting Sperm Whales again, but none that they recognized. After documenting 463 new whales and recording their codas, they realized that these were two completely new clans known as "short" and "+4," which had rarely, if ever, visited the Galápagos in the past. They were, however, known to roam the Pacific Ocean thousands of miles away. Their arrival was, therefore, unexpected. Such a cultural turnover has only really been documented in humans. As one of the researchers, Dr. Shane Gero, put it: "It's as if you had been going to Canada for 20 years, and everybody spoke English and French, and suddenly everyone packed up and left Canada for the next 10 years. When you finally went back again, everyone spoke Spanish and Portuguese." Different whales, different dialects.

Why this shift? Perhaps changes in climate resulted in a shift of resources preferred by the different clans. They adapt rather than change their preferences, allowing them to maintain their social groups, behaviors, and cultures. Alternatively, heavy whaling in the region may have redistributed surviving whales into high-quality habitats. While we might never know the answer, it is clear that these populations will likely keep moving to ensure they have access to favorable habitats, indicating that this species must be managed based on their cultural differences and not their geographical boundaries.

Some populations have started to make their way back to places where they were historically found until they were brutally hunted and reduced in numbers during the extensive whaling era. Historically, the Seychelles archipelago off the east coast of Africa was an opportunistic whaling ground for Soviet whaling fleets en route to and from the Antarctic. Between 1963 and 1966, whalers took 500 individuals from these waters alone—with the last

WHALING SHIP WITH A CAPTURED BLUE WHALE
Widespread whaling continued until well into the twentieth century.

Northern Indian Ocean Pygmy Blue Whale being taken in 1964. Yet, a few years ago, they made a comeback. Researchers heard the Sri Lankan call through the hydrophones, indicating that the population was the same as the Northern Indian Ocean Pygmy Blue Whale that was typically found within Sri Lankan waters. They were returning to this area because they recognized it as a safe space once again.

A similar moment of joy was experienced when a large Fin Whale feeding aggregation was documented off Elephant Island in the Antarctic a few years ago. While Fin Whales in the Southern Hemisphere were almost driven to extinction by twentieth-century industrial whaling, this return to ancestral feeding grounds is a sign of a recovering population. Their return in large numbers could support the restoration of crucial ecosystem functions, since they help cycle nutrients within the area.

Sei Whales are also returning to Argentina's Patagonian coast after nearly vanishing over a century ago due to relentless whaling in the 1920s and 1930s. Today, their numbers have rebounded such that they are visible once again.

Hitchhikers

While migration seems like a long and lonely journey, whales do not always travel alone. Sometimes, they are accompanied by a few friends, other times by their young, and, in yet other cases, they might be accompanied by an unlikely buddy that is there very much for the free ride.

Many slow-moving whale species are known to host encrusting parasites or barnacles, particularly on their chins and heads where water flow is consistent—an essential feature for a filter-feeding organism. Barnacles, often seen on Humpback Whale chins, are commensal organisms, not parasites—the barnacles use the whales as a stable home to hitchhike and gain access to good feeding grounds. The barnacles benefit, but there is no cost to the whale, making it quite a good arrangement. Barnacles begin their lives as microscopic larvae that move at the mercy of the ocean currents. While it is unclear how barnacles attach to whales in the first place, scientists think they have evolved to breed at the same times and in the same places as whales—in warm, shallow

BARNACLES
A Humpback Whale resplendent with barnacles.

waters. If a whale swims by a barnacle spawning site, the larvae likely attach to the whale and, in time, they truly "move in," building their hard, volcano-shaped shell homes and laying down their anchors that embed into the whale's skin so they are not removed as the skin sloughs off. As the whale migrates, the hitchhiking barnacles get a free ride from their tropical homes to plankton-rich waters where they can gorge to their heart's content.

Barnacles, however, are not just hitchhikers but also documenters of history and unknown journeys. Whale barnacles belong to a specialized family of acorn barnacles that grow unusually large—to the size of a small coffee cup. While some species of whale barnacle will attach to a few whale species, others are far pickier and attach exclusively to a single species. As the barnacles grow, they lay down rings of calcite, the most abundant natural form of calcium carbonate. As they do so, they also pull dissolved oxygen and minerals from the seawater around them. The chemical composition of the layers laid down depends on the water in which they are formed, providing insight into where the whales have been.

Remora fish also use whales, which are many times their size, to get around. However, unlike the one-way relationship between barnacles and whales, this relationship is two-way, with both parties benefiting. The remoras ride free and feed on scraps from their host while keeping the host healthy and parasite-free. While it might seem that the remoras are just latching on wherever possible, they are picky about their parking places. They choose places where they face the least resistance from the flow of water created as the whale moves: behind the whale's blowhole, behind and next to the dorsal fin, and above and behind the pectoral fin. This allows the remoras to experience up to 84 percent less drag, making it a more secure and comfortable ride. While the fleshy ring of connective tissue around the periphery of the disk is so strong that the remora could even stick to the tail fluke, where drag is the strongest, the remora stays latched on and avoids any extra energy expenditure by targeting these three spots.

Contrary to what one may think, the fish are not hanging on for dear life and can shift position even while their host is speeding along at 16 ft (5 m) per second. To do this, they skim and surf within a thin layer of fluid along the whale's skin, just over an inch thick. Called a "boundary layer," this has lower drag forces relative to the flow outside the layer, which means that when the remoras release and swim forward to reposition themselves, they are not ejected clean off their host's body into the abyss. While this may seem like an easy, almost lazy way of life, it certainly is not. Remoras do not control where they travel— they follow their hosts from the surface to bathypelagic depths (about 3,300– 9,800 ft/1,000–3,000 m), where they are exposed to extreme gradients of light, dissolved oxygen, temperature, and pressure; the adaptations that enable them to survive this journey remain a mystery.

DIVING

Of course, whales travel vertically in the ocean as well as laterally. They are uniquely adapted to dive to depth while holding their breath for extended periods. Somewhat counterintuitively, whales exhale before diving to ensure they sink faster. As they descend in search of food, many of the deeper-diving species have evolved unique adaptations. Their lungs collapse, and their flexible rib cages fold to ensure they can cope with the crushing pressures they experience as they descend. This means that only non-compressible oxygen stores in blood and muscle are used during a dive, as the whales cannot rely on lung oxygen.

Hemoglobin, a blood protein humans also possess, carries oxygen to the muscles and is transferred to myoglobin for storage. Due to their tendency to hold their breath and dive for long periods, whale myocytes are filled with high levels of myoglobin. Myoglobin is a key oxygen store; whales have higher concentrations than terrestrial mammals, including humans, ranging from 1.81 to 5.78 g per 100 g of wet muscle in whales, compared to just 0.47 g per 100 g of wet muscle in humans.

During a dive, a whale's body focuses on keeping them alive, as it should. Blood is brought to the muscles and brain to conserve heat and oxygen. Their heart rate slows down; Blue Whale heart rates can drop as low as 2 bpm, which is a 90 percent reduction compared to their surface heart rate. Non-vital systems like digestion also shut down. On the way back up, they may ascend slowly or regulate their dive patterns to avoid decompression sickness or "the bends." However, more critically, their alveoli (tiny air sacs where gas exchange happens) physically collapse under high pressure at depth, preventing further gas exchange and preventing nitrogen from entering the bloodstream, which occurs when dissolved nitrogen in the bloodstream forms bubbles in the blood and tissues due to a sudden pressure drop. As pressure decreases, the whales' lungs expand and non-vital systems kick back in.

The depths whales dive to are typically limited to the depths at which their food is found. While working on a research vessel in the North Sea a few years ago, I had an incredible moment when we were running an ROV (Remotely Operated Vehicle) at 1,200 m, documenting what seemed like an unending field of birds-nest-shaped Pheronema sponges. While in the ROV shack, I got a message saying there were Pilot Whales up top, so I rushed out to have a look. They were my first Long-finned Pilot Whales (*Globicephala melas*)—we get Short-finned Pilot Whales (*Globicephala macrorhynchus*) in Sri Lanka—and I kept wondering if they had any idea that there was a vast forest of sponges less than a mile below them. Since pilot whales have only been recorded diving to 2000 feet (600 m), I guess they didn't. But for me, this was an incredible moment. I was able to observe an immensely varied vertical slice of the ocean; it felt incredibly special.

8

WHALE SONG

Imagine you lived in an underground bunker with no lights to see and navigate. As a species dependent on vision, how would you get around? Perhaps you would adapt—reaching out in front of you as you walked to ensure you did not bump into anything or stub your toe, sniffing around to find your favorite food, or shouting out people's names so you could listen for where they might be. For whales that have evolved to live in a watery world where light penetration is limited, life in the ocean has required them to shift their investment into senses other than vision. In their case, they have evolved to "see" the world through their ears.

THE UNDERWATER SENSE— SOUND

Sound is, in fact, everything to whales. Not only do they use it to communicate with family, flirt with mates, and reprimand their young, but they also use it to avoid obstacles and find food. Sound travels farther and faster in water than in air because water particles are packed closer together. This means neighboring particles do not have to travel too far to bump into one another. As a result, sound travels about 4.3 times faster in water than it does in air, making sound the sense of choice for many underwater dwellers.

Whales are the only species, apart from humans and crows, that are known to communicate using vocal registers. In humans, these are a range of tones produced by particular vibratory patterns of the vocal folds. Whales and humans are said to have three vocal registers apiece (though humans are sometimes assigned more and the jury is out on exactly what the final number might be). A normal chest voice (which we use to speak), falsetto (which we use to sing), and vocal fry (which we use for low-pitched sounds). The latter is highly directional, meaning that the sound waves all travel in the same direction, like the beam of a flashlight. While useful in

AMBULOCETUS
This early ancestor of the whale lived both on land and in water.

echolocation for catching prey, it is not as useful for communication because the listener would have to be in the correct location to hear what is being said. The sound waves used in the chest and falsetto registers tend to spread out in every direction, allowing whales to communicate over a broader area.

Whales hear using the fatty deposits in their lower jaws. They pick up sound vibrations through their lower jaw and transmit them through fat deposits in their inner ears. The ear canals of mysticetes are likely vestigial, serving no purpose, since they are blocked with wax that is more useful for calculating age than anything else. The bones in the inner ear then conduct sound, carrying it to the cochlea, where sound waves trigger hair cells that act like messengers by sending information to the brain. Whales' advantage is that, unlike in humans, the bones in their ears are not attached to their skulls. This isolates their ears from one another and their skull, making it much easier to tell where a sound is coming from or to localize it. This is incredibly useful when trying to figure out where your prey is swimming off to. It is hard to fathom hearing things through your jaw, but if it works, it works! As it turns out, the ancient fossil ancestor of whales *Ambulocetus*, known as the "walking whale," had a large cavity in its lower jaw that likely housed the extensive fat pads used by modern whales to eavesdrop on their world.

How do baleen whales communicate?

Baleen whales, like humans, make sounds using their larynx, or voice box. But unlike us, they have evolved a unique structure: a cushion of fat and muscle inside the larynx. Despite knowing, since the 1970s, that baleen whales made beautiful, haunting songs, how they produced them remained a mystery until very recently.

The larynx is an ancient organ that evolved when the first land vertebrates started breathing air and needed to separate food from air to prevent choking and produce sound. Human vocal cords—folds within the larynx—stretch across our airways and vibrate when air from the lungs flows across them. The aryte-noids, a pair of small, pyramid-shaped cartilaginous structures at the back of the

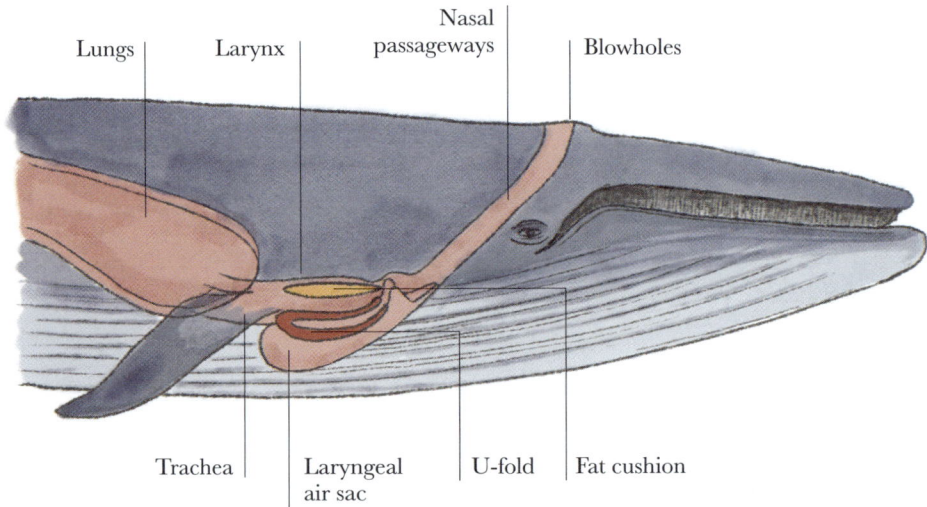

HOW BALEEN WHALES SING
Baleen whales use a unique cushion of fat inside the larynx to make their haunting melodies.

larynx, help the vocal cords to move. The arytenoids in baleen whales have transformed into a pair of elongated cylinders that fuse to form a U-shape, spanning nearly the entire length of the larynx. This rigidity is likely a means to keep their airways open when the whales need to move large quantities of air in and out of their bodies—when they reach the ocean's surface after a dive, for example. When the whales exhale, these arytenoids press against the laryngeal cushion, vibrating as air flows through, generating sound. This modification in their voice box allows them to make sounds and breathe without choking.

Blue Whales (*Balaenoptera musculus*) produce low-frequency calls packed with energy. These are less affected by scattering, distortion, and transmission loss, purportedly allowing them to be heard thousands of miles away. Their calls travel so far that, although you and I might consider Blue Whales solitary creatures, because we rarely see them swimming in pairs and even more rarely see them in any bigger groups, it is important to remember that if you were able to chinwag with your friends and family across entire ocean basins, then perhaps you would not need to be close by—within touching distance. Despite being so loud and powerful, their sounds are in the infrasonic range of around 14 Hz, which is too low for you or me to hear (our hearing range is 20–20,000 Hz). Baleen whales specialize in making low-frequency sounds like grunts and moans, with some organizing them into patterns that make up long, repeating calls or songs that males seem to use mostly in courtship (much like in songbirds).

Unfortunately, this remarkable ability to produce low-frequency, high-energy, far-ranging sounds is becoming increasingly limited in use as the oceans get noisier and noisier. As ship and boat traffic, oil and gas drilling, sonar, and other sources of noise increase in our oceans, they pose a problem for whales, as the range over which they communicate is reduced (background noise limits how far their sounds can travel). Their sounds are increasingly masked, making it impossible for the whales to communicate with one another or even find food. What happens here is similar to if you are at a party and everyone is talking at once; it is noisy, so you alter the volume of your conversation to be heard. The issue for whales is that their sound-producing organs limit how much they can shift their volumes. Ultimately, their communication ability will be affected as background noise levels increase.

How do toothed whales communicate?

Toothed whale sound production is all in the nose. They are known for their short bursts of high-frequency sounds, often repeating as pulsed calls. Some toothed whale groups have dialects—unique sets of calls they use to communicate with other individuals in their group or pod. Toothed whales also use whistles, which have a higher frequency and are continuous but can be modulated. When we are out at sea, and a pod of dolphins comes over to bowride (or swim at the front of our moving boat), we often hang out at the bow watching them as they easily slip past each other and do not so much as bump into one another. All the while, you can hear their high-frequency whistles over the surface of the water and it is clear that this is how they choreograph their fluid movements so perfectly.

Clicks are the highest-frequency sounds produced by toothed whales, and

BOW RIDING
*Dolphins often swim at the front of moving boats, using
the pressure waves created to swim effortlessly.*

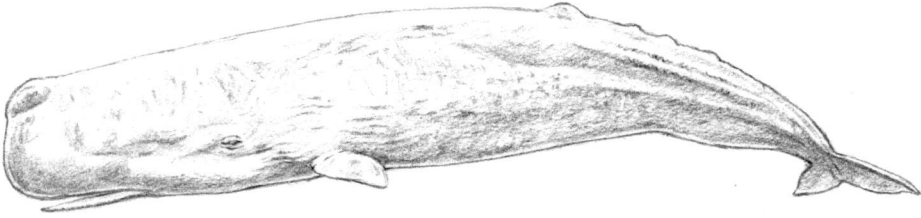

SPERM WHALE
*These whales use echolocation clicks and buzzes
to find their lunch and avoid obstacles.*

they are used for several different functions, from communication to finding prey. Echolocation clicks are a series of clicks emitted by toothed whales for prey capture or to "see" the obstacles in their path—essentially, they bounce sounds off obstacles and prey and, based on the sound received, they can calculate exactly where the prey or object is located. Toothed whales have been using this method for tens of millions of years. It all begins when they push pressurized air from their lungs toward the phonic lips in their nose—these "spare" lips, which are made up of connective tissue and fat, open for a millisecond and then snap back, creating a tissue vibration that forms a very loud click in the water in front of them. In all mammals, sound is created by the movement of air over the larynx, but while for terrestrial species air is also the medium over which the sound is propagated, for whales the medium for sound propagation changes from air to water. This click system uses little air, and that which it does use is recycled, an important feature for an animal that is about to dive deep and collapse its lungs so it does not implode. Air, after all, is precious.

Sperm Whales (*Physeter macrocephalus*) are well known for using clicks and buzzes in echolocation. Contrary to common belief, they do not use sound to kill or stun their prey—but as they approach, the intensity of their clicks

157

decreases and they grab their prey with their teeth. They also use a series of other click types for different purposes. Codas, patterned series of clicks, are used to communicate with one another, while slow clicks, or "clangs," are used exclusively by males for long-range communication on the feeding grounds, as well as on the breeding grounds where they roam between groups of females. Fascinatingly, the time between the clicks or the inter-pulse interval (IPI) can be used to estimate the size of the individual producing the sound. The IPI is the time for a pulse to travel between the air sacs at either end of a Sperm Whale's head. The bigger the head, the longer the IPI, and vice versa.

Non-vocal sounds

Communication in whales can be vocal or non-vocal in nature. Non-vocal sounds, considered a social sound repertoire, are made by males, females, and calves and can be heard in varied social and environmental contexts. Unlike whale songs, they lack any continuous pattern. One such type of non-vocal sound is surface active behavior, which includes pec slapping, tail slapping, and even breaching.

A breaching whale is truly something to behold. The sheer power generated to leap clean out of the water, often more than once, and sometimes many times over several hours, is truly hard to fathom. While I have witnessed Humpback Whales (*Megaptera novaeangliae*) breaching on many occasions, one juvenile off in the waters off Monterey, California, breached nonstop for over 45 minutes. My most incredible encounter, however, was when I observed three Humpback Whales breaching in perfect unison somewhere off the coast of Western Australia. These beautifully choreographed movements left me wondering what they were for. While most of what I had learned in university suggested that breaching was to shake off parasites or for play, the fact that they were doing it while on their lengthy migrations, mostly in a fasted state, led me to think that there must have been something more important going on. Turns out, there is!

Breaching is a very energetically expensive behavior and depends on some key things: the length of the animal (shorter animals are more maneuverable

A JUVENILE HUMPBACK WHALE BREACHING
Humpbacks are perfectly designed to breach, which they do for the sheer pleasure of it, to remove parasites, or to communicate their health and strength to others.

and require slower speeds and lower muscle power to breach), and the surface area of their flukes and flippers. The larger the surface area, the faster they can move and turn. Although a 49-ft (15-m) whale expends around ten times more energy per breach than a 26-ft (8-m) whale, and the total energy used in a single breach may match what a 132-lb (60-kg) human burns while running an entire 26.2-mile (42.2-km) marathon, this comparison doesn't capture the full picture. Due to their massive size, the relative energy cost for the whale, when expressed as a proportion of its metabolism, is far less extreme than a marathon is for a human. While breaching is energetically expensive in absolute terms, it is not nearly as taxing relative to the whale's physiology. Turns out that Humpback Whales are perfectly suited for breaching thanks to their length but also their ability to maneuver easily. While this activity requires a great effort, particularly for a whale that is not feeding, breaching is often seen on migration. This has led scientists to believe that breaching must also be a means of communication, particularly given how far sound travels in water. Given the enormous amount of energy expended with each leap and giant splash, it allows the whale to display its health and strength to peers and potential mates.

TYPES OF VOCAL SOUNDS

Surface active behaviors are just one form of whale communication in whales, but the best-known form of communication is whale song. While Humpback Whale song is used by humans for meditation and relaxation, due to its slow melodic qualities, other baleen whales also sing, and toothed whales produce whistles and clicks.

Humpback song types

Whale song is often synonymous with the hauntingly beautiful yet complex call of the Humpback Whale, made famous as part of the "Golden Record" launched into space in 1977 aboard the two *Voyager* spacecraft. A "time capsule" of sorts, the record contained a recording of a Humpback Whale song collected by Dr. Roger Payne in Bermuda in 1970.

All Humpback Whales use sound to communicate, but it is only the males that sing. That is not to say that females and calves do not communicate—but their calls are relatively short and certainly not complex, highly structured, or stereotypical like those of the males. Singing males hang motionless with their heads hanging down around 49 ft (15 m) below the ocean's surface, sometimes for hours. They come up every 20 minutes or so for a breath of air and then they return to sing, which they do with their mouths closed—just as we do when we hum. Songs are varied, with each breeding population having a different song.

Surfers and swimmers who find themselves near Humpback Whale breeding areas often report hearing whale songs when they stick their heads underwater even from a safe distance away. If the opportunity presents itself, you can try it too—and you may be greeted by the beautiful melody of one of the male singers. While we can only hear parts of the songs because they include lower frequencies outside our range of hearing, it is not hard to imagine why the females get drawn in. Perhaps Humpback Whales are the true sirens of our oceans.

Humpback Whale songs are made up of units—moans, cries, and chirps—arranged into phrases. A series of repeated phrases make themes, and a series of themes finally make up a song. This hierarchical structure is akin to a poem. If you think of each phrase as a line, and each theme as a stanza, then if you arrange multiple themes (or stanzas) together in a specific sequence, you get a poem. While at the breeding grounds, all the males sing the same current rendition of a song, sometimes even singing together in choruses. Adult male Humpbacks can sing songs for anywhere from 5 minutes to more than 24 hours, repeating the same song over and over and seemingly never getting bored.

Humpback song transfer

Humpback Whales, being "vocal production learners," can modify their songs if they are exposed to other singers and, as such, a song that is popular in one breeding season might be replaced by a new one in the next. This is unusual given that most animals are quite happy singing or vocalizing the same way forever. (Think of a dog!) Songs can change as one male adds a unit or changes a theme. In northern populations, songs are said to evolve slowly, which is likely a result of the geography. In the South Pacific, progressive cultural evolution also occurs; however, periodic cultural revolutions have led to rapid and complete replacement of one song type by another introduced from a neighboring population.

These revolutions are likely possible because individuals in the Southern Hemisphere interact with those from other ocean basins. For song to transmit between individuals of the various breeding populations, they must be within about 6 miles (10 km) of each other to hear all parts of the song, even the

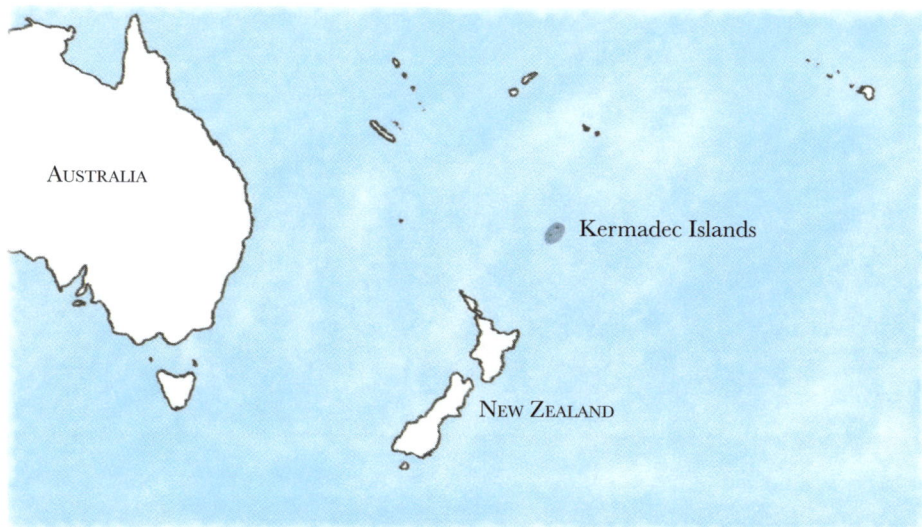

THE KERMADEC ISLANDS

These Pacific islands are a meeting place and thus a veritable melting pot of Humpback Whales from the various South Pacific breeding populations on their southward migration and visitors from the Indian Ocean.

high-frequency elements. Song can be transmitted either on a shared feeding ground—if whales switch breeding grounds either within or between seasons and they take their song with them—or it can also be shared on migratory routes. The Kermadec Islands in the northern part of New Zealand is essentially a karaoke bar with a melting pot of individuals from the various South Pacific breeding populations on their southward migration. A few foreign singers from the Indian Ocean that also happened to stop over passed on their songs to the South Pacific populations, which resulted in a cultural revolution. Also in the Kermadecs, a mashup of songs has been heard, with themes from French Polynesia and Tonga many thousands of miles away. This migratory route is one way for the singers to keep their songs fresh.

Interestingly, however, songs in the Pacific have been shown to spread from East to West. A song first heard in Western Australia transmits 4,970 miles (8,000 km) to Ecuador via Eastern Australia and French Polynesia. To get from Western to Eastern Australia it took a mere two years. A song heard in Eastern

Australia was heard in French Polynesia just three years later. Thus, songs spread from the large population in Western Australia to the smaller populations across the South Pacific but where they go next is unclear. As it turns out, population size is an essential ingredient for a revolution to emerge, and hybrid songs are heard when a whale is switching from singing the old song type to the new one, thus indicating the process of change in the song. It has shown that cultural transmission of songs happens eastward in the South Pacific and that Humpback Whales are vocally connected across the ocean basin.

Broader roles of song and other whales

Because whales sing on feeding grounds and along migratory routes, their songs may have a broader role beyond attracting mates or fending off peers. Humpbacks have also been known to "sing for their supper," so to speak, having been recorded singing while diving for prey, sometimes down to depths greater than 325 ft (100 m) and even while engaging in feeding lunges. This shows that mating displays can happen anywhere conditions are suitable—and why not? More impressive, though, is that they sing while diving and lunging for food—energetically demanding activities—indicating they can manage

MINKE WHALES ARE LESSER-KNOWN SINGERS
While their song is less elaborate than that of Humpback Whales, it still has its own peculiar beauty.

competing needs as they feed while preparing for the upcoming breeding season. Perhaps a male that can sing and forage at the same time is also sending out a signal about their fitness as a mate.

While Humpback Whale songs are some of the best studied in the underwater world, they are also a gentle reminder that we still have so much to learn. Blue, Fin (*Balaenoptera physalus*), Bowhead (*Balaena mysticetus*), and Minke (*Balaenoptera acutorostrata*) Whales also sing but none are quite as elaborate. Because of Blue Whales' elusive nature and the complexity of getting genetic samples from the animals across their distribution, their songs have been used to differentiate between populations. The Sri Lankan population, for example, has a very different call ("the Sri Lankan call") to those in the Pacific and the highest-frequency call of all Blue Whale populations—high being a very relative term. It is, in fact, their calls that led scientists to realize that the populations reemerging in the Seychelles are the same as those that use the waters around Sri Lanka. Unfortunately, since the first records of Blue Whale calls were made in the 1960s, their frequency has been decreasing worldwide, sometimes in annual, but otherwise in longer, interannual timescales. This is now also being seen in other baleen whale species, but why this happens is still unclear.

While Humpback Whale mothers whisper to their calves on the breeding grounds in an effort not to be overheard by lurking male escorts, resident fish-eating Orcas (*Orcinus orca*) are known to vocalize more when finding their prey compared to transient marine-mammal-eating Orcas. As it turns out, their preferred diets have led to different hunting strategies, and since fish do not have highly developed hearing, being chatty while trying to catch them does not result in a lost meal. However, transients remain quieter and rely on stealth to hunt prey to ensure that the seals or sea lions do not hear them coming and escape. When all is done, they do break out in chatter, perhaps boasting of their success or engaging in a version of a victory celebration.

Signature whistles

Bottlenose Dolphins (*Tursiops truncatus*) have three main types of calls. They use echolocation to find food and sense their environment, burst pulse calls for social communications (often in aggressive interactions), and whistles that are used predominantly in social communication in friendlier interactions. While 40–50 percent of the whistles produced are common to the group, the rest are very individual-specific signature whistles that they use to introduce themselves. These signature whistles develop in the first year of life through vocal learning from the mother, and for females, they remain unchanged for life. At around two–three years of age, juvenile Bottlenose Dolphins seek independence by leaving their mothers and forming juvenile groups. At around age seven, the females return to their mother's network of females. Males, on the other hand, will stick around till around ten years of age, at which point they pick their one to two favorite males with whom they form alliances. Picking carefully is important because male alliances last a lifetime, and when they first form their partnership, the males will modify their signature whistles so that they become more alike.

Signature whistles are the social glue of these fission–fusion societies, since they help maintain group cohesion, and allow dolphins to locate and recognize one another (even after a decade), maintain social bonds, and differentiate between cooperative and non-cooperative partners; the dolphins can even copy each other's signature whistles to attract one another's attention. These signature whistles are so unique that scientists off the coast of Northumberland, United Kingdom, used them to estimate the size of the local Bottlenose Dolphin population.

Signature whistles, while first described in Bottlenose Dolphins, are not exclusive to this species. They have since been identified in other dolphin species, such as Indo-Pacific Bottlenose Dolphins (*T. aduncus*), Pacific White-sided Dolphins (*Lagenorhynchus obliquidens*), Indo-Pacific Humpback Dolphins (*Sousa chinensis*), Guiana Dolphins (*Sotalia guianensis*), and Common Dolphins (*Delphinus delphis*).

Sound superhighway

The SOFAR channel, or Sound Fixing and Ranging channel, is a naturally occurring channel 1,970–3,937 ft (600–1,200 m) deep in the ocean that allows sound to travel vast distances. Essentially, it is an underwater sound superhighway. At the height of World War II, scientists successfully tested their hypothesis

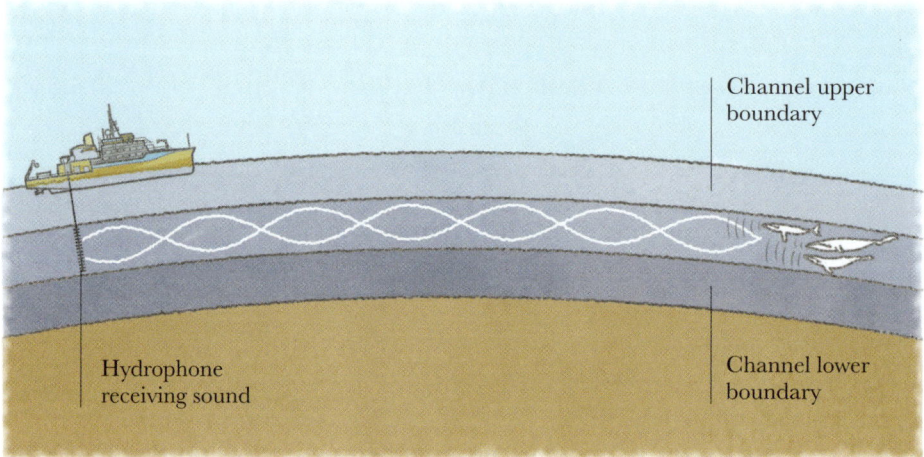

THE SOFAR CHANNEL
This naturally occurring channel deep in the ocean allows sound to travel vast distances.

that low-frequency sound traveled great distances—in the case of their experiment, 900 miles (1,450 km)—in the deep ocean. So how does this channel work?

Sound travels at different speeds in different layers of the ocean. At the surface, where water is warmer, sound travels fastest, but as you go deeper, water gets increasingly cold and sound begins to slow down. Go deep enough (~3,280 ft/~1,000 m) and the ocean temperature hits its minimum. This is where pressure starts to take over and sound speeds increase again in the deeper water. Strangely, the layer where sound travels the slowest is also where it can travel the farthest. So if a sound enters this layer at the right angle or is produced in this layer, it can get trapped within the channel and because there is no loss at the surface or absorption by the seafloor, the sound waves will continue to bend up and down and up and down and travel vast distances along this horizontal layer.

Whales have been using this SOFAR channel like a long-distance telephone to communicate with loved ones and soon-to-be loved ones across ocean basins for longer than we have known it existed. Today, hydrophones in the SOFAR channel let us eavesdrop on all the sounds in the ocean, from nuclear tests to those of whales.

A calling that turned one way then another

My first foray into the world of marine mammal research was as an under-graduate at St. Andrews University, Scotland, in 2002, when I embarked on a research project on coda calls of Sperm Whales from the Gulf of Mexico and the Azores. I remember listening to hours of recordings, trying to distinguish calls from noise and identify how many individuals were creating the cacopho-ny hitting my ears. It was only after I became familiar with these calls that I had the privilege to see my first whale, also a Sperm Whale, off Kaikoura, New Zealand, five months later. After three or four attempts, thanks to bad luck with the weather (a good glimpse into my future), I finally set eyes on a large male out in the distance and could not help but think just how small it was relative to the giant mountains in the background.

Four months after this encounter I wangled my way onto a research vessel working in the Maldives and traveling onward to Sri Lanka to study Sperm Whales and the toxicology of the ocean environment. We towed hydrophones (underwater microphones) behind our vessel at all times, recording everything

SPERM WHALE SURFACING
A lone sperm whale prepares to dive off Kaikoura, New Zealand.

we heard. While they would attract the attention of fishers and require me, as the only local Sri Lankan onboard, to communicate clearly about what they did and why we were towing them, they sucked me deeper into the world of whale acoustics. The sounds being picked up were played on loudspeakers in the pilot house, so the soundtrack of our lives was the distinctive clicking of Sperm Whales, which were the most predominant and easily recognizable calls. At this point, I wanted to continue in acoustics and I wanted to learn more about the whales by eavesdropping on their lives. Alas, it was not meant to be, and the odds were not in my favor. However, it was on this same trip that I had my encounter with Blue Whales off southern Sri Lanka, which sent me on the journey of a lifetime. I guess it's a good reminder that while not everything may go your way or as you expect or want it to, other adventures await, and if you stick with it, other doors might open and greater opportunities may be yours.

9

WHALES
AND US

When we reflect on relations between humans and whales, we are confronted by the harsh truth that our interactions have largely not been something to be proud of. Today, some people are trying to make amends for this. In simple terms, humans decimated whale populations, reducing numbers by 90 percent from pre-industrial levels. The story of whaling is complex, but without it, any story of whales would be incomplete. However, it is not the only way our lives are intertwined with those of whales. In some parts of the world whales steal from fishing lines, which can lead to conflict; in others, they are used as bait for fisheries, while in yet others, humans have learnt the value of cooperating with dolphins to catch more fish. Our interactions are many, and in some instances they may captivate us.

Whaling's early beginnings

While most of us are aware that whaling has a reasonably long (and bloody) history, few know how far back it all began. It is acknowledged that the Norwegians started non-commercial whaling in the ninth or tenth century, and commercial whaling began in the eleventh century in the Basque country in southwest Europe. However, in the Blombos cave, on the southern Cape coastline of Southern Africa, the faunal record indicates that during the Middle Stone Age, which began 280,000 years ago and ended 50–25,000 years ago, human's subsistence strategies (as indicated by found remains) included dolphins and whales. While these whales were most certainly scavenged when they washed up on the beaches, it indicates that our intertwined history has been longer than we often imagine. There is a petroglyph from southern Korea dating back to the Neolithic (6000 BCE) depicting whales tethered to boats by ropes (and maybe harpoons). In 1850, archaeologists in Skara Brae, Scotland, unearthed a figure carved out of whalebone called a Buddo, a non-gendered human from 2900–2400 BCE. While it is unclear if the whalebone was acquired through hunting or scavenging, it also points to a long-standing relationship between our two species.

For the Basque whalers, however, the target was the North Atlantic Right Whales (*Eubalaena glacialis*) in the Bay of Biscay, which they hunted for meat and other prod-

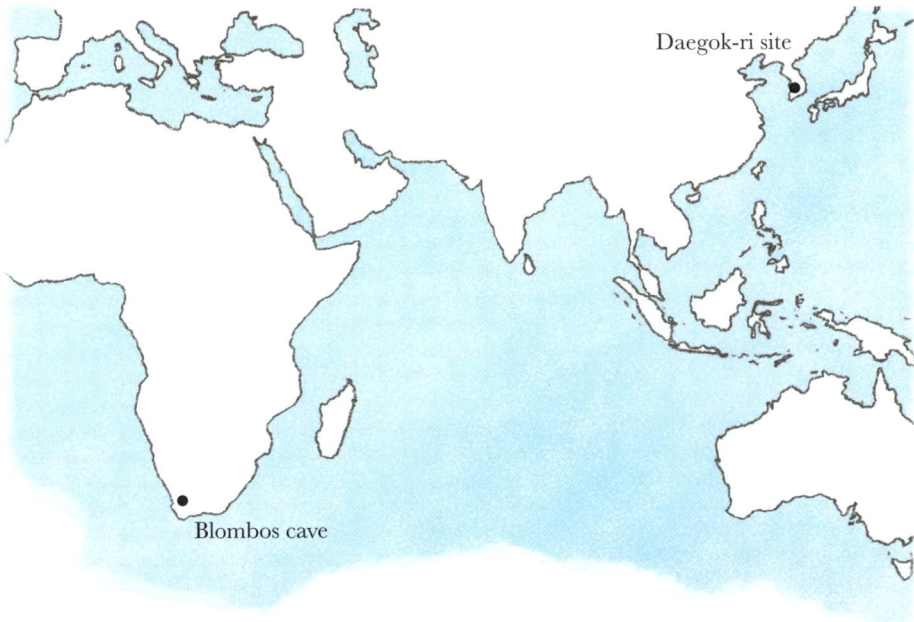

HUMAN–WHALE ENCOUNTERS
Some of the earliest evidence of human–whale interactions comes from the
Blombos cave in South Africa and from the Daegok-ri site in South Korea.

ucts that could be traded. With the addition of oceangoing ships to their fleet, whalers expanded their operations from Ireland in the fourteenth century to the North Atlantic in the sixteenth century (the whaling station in Red Bay, Canada, is now a UNESCO World Heritage site) and Iceland in the seventeenth century.

Whaling: 1800s to 1970s

From roughly the late seventeenth to the late nineteenth century, Yankee whalers from Nantucket, off the East Coast of the U.S., extracted oil from whales they hunted close to shore and brought ashore to be processed. It proved a lucrative business, and the whalers soon shifted to boat-based operations in the 1690s to capture Right Whales. In these times, whaling was an extraordinarily dangerous business, both physically and economically—death being a common result of the tussle between human and beast. Men yielding hand-held harpoons and killing lances hunted whales from small open boats. The hand-thrown harpoon was only good enough to attach a rope to the whale but not kill it. Once wounded, the

171

whale would become angry and start flailing violently. Known as the "Nantucket sleigh ride," the whalers would then be dragged along by the angry whale desperately trying to rid itself of the pain. These coastal operations were so efficient that by the mid-1700s, finding Right Whales along the Atlantic coast of North America became increasingly difficult. For whalers, it was time to move further afield in search of Sperm Whales (*Physeter macrocephalus*).

By the 1800s, Yankee whalers had famously started to hunt Sperm Whales in the South Atlantic, Pacific, and Indian Oceans using bigger ships. All this, for what? Oil. An average-sized Sperm Whale would yield 25–40 barrels of coveted oil extracted from its blubber. Even in the most extreme temperatures, it retained its lubricating qualities, making it perfect for use with machinery; it burned bright without smoke and odor, making it ideal for lamps; and as an oil byproduct, soap was produced. Spermaceti oil extracted from the head of the sperm whale also burned bright and clear, making it perfect for the highest-quality candles. Demand for this oil continued even after Yankee whaling ceased, only declining when the oil of the jojoba plant was found to be a better substitute for high-friction applications—at which point the price of sperm whale oil dropped by a drastic 90 percent.

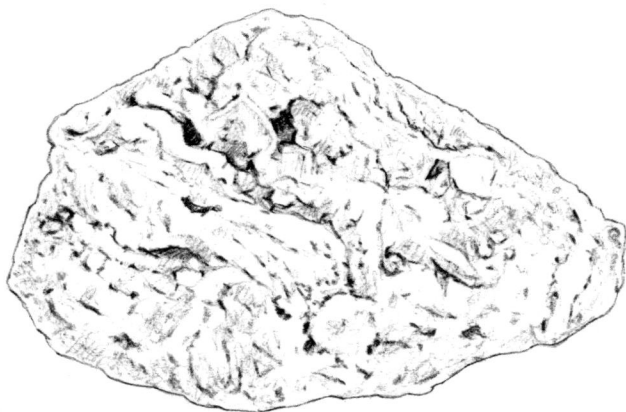

AMBERGRIS
In its dried form, ambergris has a solid, waxy texture and can range in color from light gray to brown.

However, whale oil extracted from the blubber of Right, Bowhead (*Balaena mysticetus*), and Humpback (*Megaptera novaeangliae*) Whales, despite being of lower quality, was still valuable for illumination and as a lubricant. Whalers also found other parts of the whale useful for nineteenth-century society. Baleen, those long fibrous, comb-like structures that hang from the roofs of whales' mouths, were used extensively for corset stays, hoops for women's skirts, umbrella ribs, fishing poles, buggy whips, and carriage springs. Ambergris, the wax-like substance that forms around sharp squid beaks in Sperm Whale stomachs in order to protect the whale's digestive system—is still occasionally used today. It is found exclusively in Sperm Whales, but crucially, not all Sperm Whales produce it. Unfortunately this is not always appreciated, and in some countries, any time a whale washes up dead on a beach it is cut into by people hoping to find what was once known as "liquid gold." Ambergris is in fact worth *more* than its weight in gold, and the largest piece ever found weighed half a ton (450 kg), which is almost as much as a small car! It is so valuable because it contains the compound ambrein, that likely gives the substance its sweet, musky scent and helps stabilize other scents. The classic scent of Chanel No. 5 is, in part, thanks to ambergris.

In the early days, the Blue Whale (*Balaenoptera musculus*) was safe from the hands of the whalers due to its speed and because its carcass would sink, thanks to being negatively buoyant. Right Whales, on the other hand, were the *right* whales to kill (see page 19)—slow and buoyant, so once harpooned, they would float at the surface, their carcass waiting for pick-up. Unfortunately, the invention of the steam-powered whaling ship in 1863 and the exploding deck-mounted harpoon (which exploded inside the whale) by Norwegian shipping magnate Svend Foyn, called the "father of modern whaling," in 1870 revolutionized whaling and paved the way for a more prosperous modern industry. Mounted on the bow of a whale catcher, this harpoon was fast—it could outpace a Blue Whale—and because it was tethered, the whale was then attached to the boat with no chance of escape, giving the whalers sufficient time to approach and inflate the carcass so that it would float, and not sink to the bottom of the ocean before they proceeded with their duties.

BLUE WHALE
The Blue Whale is the largest animal ever known to have existed on Earth.

Blue Whales became the most sought-after because a single 90-ft (27-m) animal could yield up to 120 barrels of oil. As such, they were killed in the thousands (over 29,000 in the 1931 season alone). Catches were so high that when world production increased between the 1928 and 1929 and the 1930 and 1931 seasons, soap and margarine were produced in such abundance that it was more than could be used by the entire world. After this, Blue Whales became so scarce that whalers turned to other species.

From 1900 to 1999, it is estimated that the whaling industry killed 2.9 million whales, in what is considered the largest cull of any animal, in terms of total biomass, in human history. Blue Whales were depleted by 90 percent, and Sperm Whales were driven down to one-third of their pre-whaling numbers. In the early whaling years, sail-powered whaling ships took around 300,000 Sperm Whales. With the advent of technology, twentieth-century whalers matched the previous two centuries of sperm whale destruction in just over 60 years, with the same number being hunted again in the following decade. Factory ships introduced before World War I carried small aircraft for whale spotting. Their immense size and capacity replaced shore-based stations, allowing whalers the freedom to roam farther afield. After World War II, huge factory ships were built, further increasing access and ability to stay out at sea. Whaling began to decline at the end of the twentieth century. The decline of the Yankee whaling fleet coincided with the discovery of oil in the ground in the 1860s, but the main driver for the end of industrial whaling included the emergence of affordable alternatives to industrial whaling products such as margarine, soap, cosmetics, meat, and oil lubricants; a critically depleted resource from massive overfishing of whales; and the resulting rising global conservation ethic.

The International Whaling Commission

In 1931, the introduction of the International Convention for the Regulation of Whaling set out regulations for managing whale stocks, which included the conservation and utilization of whale species. In 1946, the International Whaling Commission (IWC) was established under this convention to oversee whale stocks and the development of whaling. However, described as the "whalers' club," they failed to safeguard whales in their first three decades, during which time several species were driven to the brink of extinction.

The IWC introduced the Blue Whale Unit (BWU), a quota system used to regulate whaling based on the amount of oil extracted from one Blue Whale

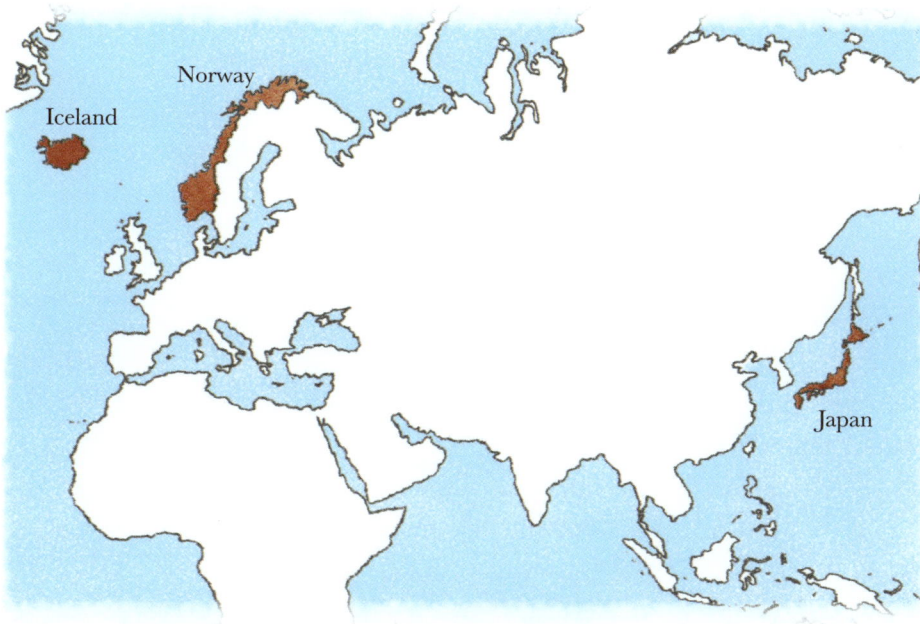

MODERN WHALING
Today, only a few countries—such as Japan, Iceland, and Norway—engage in whaling.

compared to other species. The conversion went as follows: One Blue Whale unit equalled two Fin Whales (*Balaenoptera physalus*), two and a half Humpback Whales, or six Sei Whales (*B. borealis*). This system has been highly criticized for encouraging the sequential depletion of species from the biggest to the smallest, ignoring the impact on individual populations of each species and considering all whales as a collective commodity. By 1971, when they finally set species- and area-specific catch limits, the Blue Whales were all but gone.

With plummeting population numbers, the IWC put into place a moratorium in 1982, which came into force in 1986, and declared two whale sanctuaries in the Indian Ocean and Southern Ocean, where commercial whaling was completely banned. Unfortunately, the commercial ban applies only to countries that are part of the IWC, and the IWC has no regulations for scientific whaling. Countries like Japan have previously exploited this "scientific whaling" loophole for several decades. Eventually, they left the IWC and chose to whale in their own coastal waters. Norway registered an objection to the moratorium, and Iceland lodged a reservation against it, allowing them to continue to hunt whales even today. Over time, the IWC went from an authority that managed the utilization of stocks to one that prioritized the conservation of these same species. Today, the IWC's scientific committee is heralded as the greatest repository of cetacean scientific knowledge.

Social learning saves Sperm Whales

While whalers were successful in all but wiping out most species of cetaceans, the story of whaling would be incomplete without mention of how Sperm Whales' ability to pass on knowledge might have saved them from extinction, at least in the North Pacific. Researchers noticed that the number of Sperm Whales being hunted in the North Pacific by the Yankee whalers started to decline around the 1820s and decided to investigate the cause using archived logbook data. As it turned out, in the first year or so, every whale spotted was captured by the whalers but, within three to four years, the whalers lamented about the increasing difficulty in catching the whales they would find, with a 58 percent drop in success.

In the early years, naïve whales had never met and developed defenses against the open-boat whalers who flung harpoons to catch them. However, over time, the naïve social units rapidly learned effective defense mechanisms from those with experience, allowing them to dodge whalers. Key to this was that the whales stopped doing what they used to do, like aggregating, a behavior displayed by Sperm Whales when threatened by their natural predator, Orcas (*Orcinus orca*). Instead, they would alarm each other, flee (particularly upwind, which made it difficult for the rowboats to catch up to them), do deep dives to get out of the way, and attack the whalers, whose boats were far from robust. Frustrated whalers described all of these behaviors, and the precise documentation provides insight into the power of culture in maintaining Sperm Whale populations in the North Pacific during peak Yankee whaling years.

Subsistence hunting

In some communities, particularly remote regions where winters are harsh and food can be scarce, Aboriginal peoples have hunted whales to meet their

ATLANTIC WHITE-SIDED DOLPHINS
These dolphins continue to be hunted in the Faroe Islands.

cultural and nutritional needs for a very long time. The survival of an entire community can depend on the whales they catch, which they do thoughtfully and in moderate numbers. Alaska Natives and Canadian Inuit communities depend on subsistence hunting of Bowhead Whales for survival. More recently, Russian sub-hunters have acquired the right to hunt whales from the Bering–Chukchi-Beaufort Seas, while Greenland, St. Vincent, and the Grenadines are also known to engage in subsistence hunting.

The Faroe Islands have engaged in a subsistence hunt known as "The Grindadráp," (or the Grind) since the sixteenth century, which continues to see Long-finned Pilot Whales (*Globicephala melaena*), Atlantic White-sided Dolphins (*Lagenorhynchus acutus*), and Bottlenose Dolphins (*Tursiops truncatus*) herded into bays by locals on powerboats and jet skis. Licensed individuals then sever the spinal cord and the associated blood vessels using a long-handled lance, which is said to ensure near-instantaneous unconsciousness and death. The water runs red as families of these highly social species are killed. The meat is then distributed amongst those who participated in the hunt and is considered an important source of protein for the islanders. This hunt, more than others, has been called out for its inhumane practices, with many citing that herding and trapping the animals leads to high levels of distress, while the severing of the spinal cord does not result in instantaneous death.

In Lamalera, Indonesia, the hunt for Sperm Whales with handheld harpoons continues. The Lamaleran community living on the western end of Lembata Island turned to whaling because of the lack of year-round streams and inhospitable rocky terrain around their homes, which prevented agriculture. As they looked out from their cliffs at the strait below, the Lamalerans saw marine animals that could sustain them. While they hunt dolphins, mantas, sharks, turtles, and swordfish, only the Sperm Whales are sacred to the community, summoned during a ritual called "the calling of the whales."

Some say that subsistence whaling with bamboo harpoons, wooden boats (though some now use boats with outboard engines), and inflight acrobatics has continued for five centuries, making it physically and spiritually important to the community. Sperm Whales are used in their entirety, including

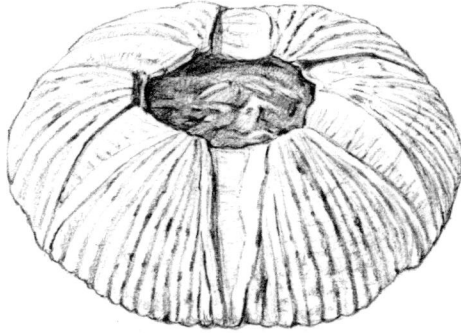

CETOPIRUS COMPLANATUS
This whale barnacle fossil was discovered off the Mediterranean coast of Spain in 2017.

their eyeballs, brain, and oil. With 20 taken a year, whale meat is also used as currency in the barter economy the hunters share with communities in other parts of Lembata Island that live in the wetter, mountainous, more agriculture-friendly areas, allowing them to "buy" rice, cassava, and other vegetables. A 6-in (15-cm) strip of whale jerky buys them about a dozen bananas. In 2000, anthropologists studying traditional societies worldwide found that Lamalerans were the most generous at distributing resources amongst the community, indicating a highly mutualistic society. While at one point this hunt became a tourist attraction, with pro-whaling tourists paying to attend, today, due to efforts to ban this hunt in favor of tourism, the villagers have banned people from visiting their village, highlighting the need for sensitivity when addressing conservation issues.

If we have learnt anything from the whales, it is that cultures are important, but they can evolve based on the changes around us. Similarly, with many of the cultures and traditions involving humans and whales, perhaps there is a way to ensure that those traditions are honored but brought into a modern era, so that those communities can continue to thrive and survive without feeling threatened. Perhaps we can understand and empathize with both sides while seeking ways to do better in this modern world, where we know that the survival of these species will only ensure a better planet for all of us.

The loss of dependents

Since *Cetopirus complanatus*, a kind of barnacle, was known to attach exclusively to Right Whales, it was also an indicator of where Right Whales had roamed. While there are no Right Whales in the Mediterranean today, likely as a result of broader ecosystem impacts, including the disappearance of their predators (Orcas) and a reduction in marine primary productivity, the discovery of this barnacle off the Mediterranean coast of Spain in 2017 tells us that the whales roamed there once upon a time. Unfortunately, this species of barnacle has not been documented in 170 years. While researchers have spent decades desperately trying to save the whales, little thought has gone to those species that have evolved to live exclusively alongside or even on them. Charismatic megafauna does sometimes cast a shadow on smaller, "less captivating" species, which is problematic given they play important roles, as all species do, in our ecosystem. These silent extinctions can shift ecosystems in ways we do not yet understand.

Depredation

As we continue to overexploit fish stocks worldwide, fishing techniques change and adapt while whales and other marine animals must change their food-finding behaviors, resulting in conflict. In spaces where they overlap, whales, particularly toothed whales like the Northern Bottlenose Whale (*Hyperoodon ampullatus*), Sperm Whales, and Orcas, are known to steal fish from fishing gear ranging from purse seines to trawls, gillnets, pots, and baited longlines.

One particular fishery, the baited longline fishery, where fishers run many miles of monofilament lines with baited hooks hanging off them, is a particular target, especially for Sperm Whales, which are known to steal fish off the hooks for an easy meal. This behavior, known as depredation, is a must-see, as the Sperm Whales, despite their large noses and disproportionately sized mouths, nimbly remove the fish off the hooks for their own consumption.

Depredation results in socioeconomic losses for the fishers; they lose their catch and sometimes their gear and have to stay at sea longer because they do

WHALE DEPREDATION OF FISHING VESSEL CATCHES IS WIDESPREAD
Even whales as large as Orcas can become bycatch through their interactions with fisheries.

not achieve their quotas, which also results in higher fuel consumption. At the same time, it also has ecological consequences, such as whales getting caught in gear as bycatch or not being able to account for the fish stolen when estimating how much fish is caught annually to understand our exploitation rates. Depredation by Sperm Whales is truly ocean basin-wide, as they target Pacific halibut and sablefish in the North Pacific, Greenland halibut in the North Atlantic, and Patagonian toothfish in the Southern Ocean. To understand the level of loss due to depredation, a study conducted over eight years in the Crozet and Kerguelen islands in the Southern Ocean estimated that 61 percent of 5,260 longline sets (each set is one fishing attempt), equivalent to about 702 tons (637 tonnes) of losses (at a minimum) occurred in the Crozet Islands over this period, while in the Kerguelen Islands 41 percent of 16,902 sets, resulting in minimum losses of 2,649 tons (2,400 tonnes), was depredated on by Sperm Whales. While efforts have been made to decrease depredation through physical and acoustic deterrents, success is yet to come.

Adult male Bottlenose Dolphins often interact with crab pots in St. John's River, Florida, USA. Many are repeat offenders, and most are residents. Most dolphins here are in poor body condition, likely due to large-scale dredging that has shifted their habitat. The increased foraging pressure has resulted in lower-body conditions and a need to find food innovatively, including depredating crab pots.

Orcas, too, can be seen depredating, often becoming caught as bycatch in the Bering Sea trawl fisheries. A practice known as "halibut deck sorting" might be to blame, because the trawl vessels are allowed to throw accidentally caught halibut back into the sea due to restrictions on their catch. If the fish are discarded within 35 minutes and in good shape, they survive. However, the Orcas have realized that the stunned fish make an easy lunch and, they are often seen swimming with the boats. Unfortunately, this interaction has led to their bycatch, with as many as ten females being caught in 2023. Scientists speculate that this could be driven by a lack of Chinook salmon in the Bering Sea as well as the slinky pots (lightweight, collapsible traps designed to keep whales from snacking on fishers' catches) that have been introduced as an alternative to hooks to prevent Orca depredation, which result in the whales shifting their focus to the trawl boats. Ultimately, it is clear that Orcas are incredibly innovative, and one tool cannot outsmart them for long, highlighting the need for us to innovate alongside them continually.

Bait and bushmeat

A 2019 study showed that global consumption of whales and dolphins is on the rise, with about 100,000 small whales, dolphins, and porpoises from at least 56 species being intentionally hunted annually. The bushmeat trade involves the hunting of terrestrial and marine animals, including mammals and other marine species, for consumption and non-food purposes (like medicines). In the past, blame was largely placed on poorer countries that had exhausted traditional protein supplies (due to their dependency on fish exports to sustain their economy rather than it all being consumed locally).

However, it turns out that countries like Australia, the USA, Canada, and South Korea, all considered developed, also consume bushmeat. While there has been much media attention on stopping large-scale whale hunts, this increase in consumption indicates that it is not just the larger whales, but many of the smaller species that are also at risk.

In West Africa, the removal of fish by foreign vessels, mostly Chinese, has led to a decreased catch for local fishers, leading them to turn to aquatic bushmeat. In Sri Lanka, a country that historically revered the dolphin, believing that they protected fishers at sea, consumption has increased, and 15 species are eaten as bushmeat. Overfishing in these waters has also resulted in smaller fish catches for fishers. As a result, the fishers herd and catch dolphin pods while at sea to cover the costs of their fishing trips, chunking them up to prevent detection, as they are a protected species in the island's waters. Fishers know that the illegal trade in bushmeat will bring them the money they need—and over time, this practice has grown from incidental catch to a targeted one.

HECTOR'S DOLPHINS
*Some of the smallest dolphins in the world, they are now
protected and are no longer used as bait in fisheries.*

The concerns around bushmeat consumption are twofold: the impact on the target species' populations, and human health. These apex predators hunted for their meat have, over time, concentrated pollutants such as mercury in their tissues due to their position in the food chain (the higher up you go, the more concentrated things become). When consumed by humans, the ingested pollutants are further concentrated. Mercury levels are estimated to be 3–48 times above the threshold the World Health Organization considers safe.

It is important, however, to also understand that the hunt is not always driven by protein requirements. In some places, the blubber and flesh of these small cetaceans are used as bait on hooks. While much of the focus on fishery interactions with dolphins has been on bycatch, much less attention has been placed on using dolphins as bait in various fisheries, a now widespread behavior occurring in at least 33 countries across 6 continents since 1970. In some cases, the use of aquatic mammals as bait is also linked to bycatch. While many fishers will discard bycatch because that is not their target species, others may retain it as bait to enhance their harvest. Once seen to be useful as bait, there is potential for it to become a target of the fishery. Often, cetaceans are used as bait in longlines in shark fisheries—and they are not always acquired incidentally.

While widespread, in some parts of the world, the use of cetaceans as bait in fisheries has decreased. For example, a traditional fishery in the Maldives called *Maa keyolhu kan* depended on cetacean bait; however, when demand decreased due to the introduction of longlines in the 1960s, and the Maldivian government recognized the importance of sharks for tourism and banned their capture, trade, and exploitation in any form, the use of dolphins as bait completely disappeared. In New Zealand, Hector's Dolphins (*Cephalorhynchus hectori*) were used as bait in the rock lobster fishery, but this, too, has shifted due to a change in the public's perceptions of marine mammals and the introduction of the New Zealand Marine Mammals Protection Act in 1978.

LESS USUAL HUMAN–WHALE INTERACTIONS

There are other stories about the relationship between humans and whales that are less known and rarely told. Whether it is dolphins helping fishers catch more, whales spending hours right by boats, or driving unnatural behaviors in wild populations, their world has more to explore.

Historical examples of cooperative fishing

Uncle Tom was a famous Orca that cooperatively hunted with whalers in Eden Bay in New South Wales, Australia, in the late 1920s. He was full grown and weighed 6 tons (5.4 tonnes) and measured 22 ft (6.7 m). Uncle Tom led one of the pods that herded passing baleen whales into the bay and alerted whalers before partaking in the chase himself. He would swim to the mouth of the bay and tail slap to signal to the whalers that a whale was in the vicinity. Sometimes, he would participate in the chase, towing the vessel by grabbing the rope with his teeth, as evidenced by the distinctive patterns of wear and tear on the teeth of his lower jaw. Other times, he would grab the harpoon rope attached to a whale to be towed around by the injured animal.

After the whale's death, whalers would attach marker buoys and anchors to the carcass and leave it for a day or two. Within that time, the Orcas, including Uncle Tom, would take the carcass to the seafloor and eat the lips and tongue (this specificity is not unlike Orca behaviors today that involve hours' long hunts that end with just the liver or tongue of the prey being taken), after which the bloated carcass would float back to the surface and be towed to the whaling station. This ritual was called the "Law of the Tongue." Unfortunately, Old Tom starved to death after losing two teeth in a tussle over a baleen whale carcass with a local man named John Logan (who, wracked with guilt, ultimately funded the construction of the Eden Killer Whale Museum), and his carcass was found floating in the bay on September, 17, 1930. While most Orcas pass down their hunting strategies through the generations, this collaboration, often considered one of the most extraordinary mutualistic relationships ever documented, ended with Old Tom's death and his family's subsequent departure.

Early records also point to Aboriginal Australians in Moreton Bay using dolphins to frighten fish, particularly mullet and tailor, driving them toward the eagerly awaiting fishers. The fishers would call the dolphins by "jobbing" their spears into the sand under the water; this would make a "queer noise," which may have been an effort to imitate the sound of mullet splashing into the water after jumping. They would then run into the water with spears and jab at the fish, catching one or two on the spear at a time. The dolphins would swim in the chaos, catching the fish that were rounded up but had escaped the spear and sometimes being rewarded with a fish straight off the spear. Cooperative fishing between Aboriginal Australians and Orcas or Bottlenose Dolphins was geographically widespread on Australia's east coast and had an emotional and spiritual significance beyond just food acquisition. Early accounts of associations between humans and dolphins also suggest that Orcas assisted and protected people in the water, chased away sharks, and even helped swimmers when tired by slipping their fins under their arms until a launch would pick them up.

Modern cooperative fishing

Today, few examples of successful human–whale mutualistic relationships exist. Yet while dolphins are often seen as competitors to fishers, one small town in Brazil called Laguna has a different story. For more than 140 years, starting in the nineteenth century, fishers and dolphins in this area have engaged in cooperative fishing, resulting in mutual benefits for everyone—except the fish.

Resident Lahille's Bottlenose Dolphins (*Tursiops truncatus* or *Tursiops gephyreus*—subject to ongoing taxonomic debate) initiate and control the fishery and, like in Uncle Tom's case, alert the fishers to the presence of fish. They herd mullet, an important food source for local people, and drive them toward a line of ready fishers standing in knee-deep water along the shore. Once the fish are compacted, the dolphins signal with head or tail slaps or sudden deep dives in front of the fishers, indicating when and where they should cast their

LAHILLE'S BOTTLENOSE DOLPHIN
*These dolphins collaborate with humans in Laguna, Brazil,
herding mullet toward waiting lines of fishers*

nets. When dolphins arrive, the fishers rapidly move into the water and cast their nets at a higher rate than when the dolphins are not around. The mullet attract the dolphins, which attract the humans. The nets falling into the water disrupt fish schools, isolating individual fish that are then snapped up by nearby dolphins—a small tax for all their hard work. By working in synchrony, the dolphins and humans benefit. The traditional net-casting fishers are 17 times more likely to catch mullet, which they catch more of (four times, in fact) than when dolphins are not present, resulting in little conflict between the species.

This form of cooperative fishing in Laguna has existed for over a century and is part of the culture of the fishing community, passed on through social learning. While nothing in the environment stops other dolphins from participating, those relying on alternative food sources tend to depend on different lagoon areas that overlap with other fisheries' activities. Some of these activities might be illegal, leading to dolphin entanglement. The cooperative dolphins have a lower likelihood of entanglement in fishing nets, leading to an increased survival rate of 13 percent compared to their non-cooperating peers, as their

IRRAWADDY DOLPHIN
These charismatic dolphins remain critically endangered.

likelihood of entanglement in fishing nets decreases. In Laguna, just 20 dolphins support some 200 fishers with no other source of income, highlighting this relationship's important economic and social value.

Protecting this unique culture is important to prevent its loss. Unfortunately, mullet populations in Laguna are in decline due to rising ocean temperatures. Dropping mullet numbers may lead to reduced benefits for cooperation, which puts this partnership at risk as each species begins to lose interest in it. Fewer cooperative dolphins could also lead to more dolphin deaths as they encounter illegal nets or attempt to snag fish from the nets of non-cooperative fishers. Therefore, protecting mullet populations is at the center of ensuring the persistence of this unique culture.

In Myanmar, a similar cooperative fishery between the critically endangered Irrawaddy Dolphin (*Orcaella brevirostris*) in the Irrawaddy River and local fishers is at risk because of destructive fishing practices and an ongoing war. Here, fishers tap the side of their small two-person canoes rhythmically with a conical wooden pin, slap the water's surface with the flat end of their paddle, make a tinkling sound with the lead weights of their cast net on the deck of the boat, use a guttural, throaty call similar to the sound of a turkey, and make practice net casts to assess the willingness of the dolphins to cooperate. If willing, the dolphins begin to herd the fish by swimming in ever-tightening semi-circles toward the fishers. One dolphin will then signal by pushing its tail flukes toward the fisher, which is a cue to cast, and the fishers cast their nets between the boat and the dolphins. Again, fish that are separated by the chaos of the net make an easy meal for the dolphins. Dynamiting and electro-fishing are both threatening the populations of these river dolphins. At the same time, the ongoing war interferes with the efforts of local groups like the "Dolphin Guardians" to monitor population numbers (in 2020, the population in Myanmar was estimated at 79) and report illegal fishing.

Unhealthy whale interactions with humans

In the Ashtamudi Estuary, Kerala, on the southwest coast of India, fishers cast their nets off the sea walls in the presence of another dolphin species. Indo-Pacific Humpback Dolphins (*Sousa chinensis*) are considered near-threatened across their range. Like in Brazil and Myanmar, these dolphins drive fish from the deep to the shallows and signal to the fishers, who cast their nets. The dolphins catch a few fish that try to evade the cast nets in a panic. Once again, the diversity of the fisher catch is higher when they cooperate, so this partnership is a no-brainer. Unlike in the other two examples, however, the relationship is not mutually beneficial, because the fishers steal the fish from the dolphins. As such, this is considered a kleptoparasitic interaction, where only one animal benefits—the human. Kleptoparasitism is thought to be the precursor of human–wildlife cooperation if the dolphins can figure out how to coordinate their foraging with the fishers' actions and gain a benefit by snagging a big meal from the interaction in the longer term. While this evolution will take time, trawler traffic and other motorized boats threaten the dolphins in this locality. At present, around 100 fishers depend on this fishery for their primary source of income. The question remains: Will this turn into a cooperative fishery in time to save the dolphins?

Flipping the script, there are examples where dolphins associate with humans purely to access an easy meal. In Monkey Mia, Western Australia, wild Bottlenose Dolphins have been habituated and hand-fed since the 1950s. Here, the dolphins play no role in obtaining food, since they are fed by humans. While a tourism draw, this dependence has led to various issues for the dolphins, including high infant mortality, low juvenile (post-weaning) survival, and changes in their behaviors.

Mugging

In quite a different story, in the Gulf of St. Lawrence, off Canada, a male Humpback Whale called Meduse (because of the jellyfish-like scar on his tail fluke) was known to have a "thing" for the blue RHIB (rigid-hulled inflatable boat) that researchers from the Mingan Island Cetacean Study (MICS) would head out on. While there were two such RHIBs that looked exactly the same to the researchers, Meduse knew the difference between them and could often be seen making a beeline for his favorite one and lying under it for what seemed like hours on end—coming up every so often to take a breath off the side of the boat and then submerging gently right below it once again. One time, Meduse came for a visit with a female called Skateboard (so named for the skateboard-shaped scar on her fluke) in tow. Skateboard had not been seen in the Gulf in several years, so researchers were excited for her safe return and hopeful of a partnership between her and Meduse. Unfortunately, Meduse soon spotted his favorite blue boat and abandoned her to visit. Soon after, Skateboard, feeling curious, moved swiftly to investigate this paramour, only for Meduse to swim over to her, shove her aside, and return to his position under the boat.

While this may sound unusual, mugging, where roles are reversed, and the whales "people watch" and choose to interact with the boat, swimming around and under the boat and staying close for a sustained period, is not uncommon amongst Humpback Whales. The term sounds harsh, but is appropriate because these encounters make you feel like you are being held up (even though no money is lost in the process), since they can go on for long periods, some-

MUGGING
A kayaker being "mugged" by a humpback whale.

times well over an hour. People often describe feeling trapped, as a Humpback Whale will approach their research boats very close, face first, and sit there, making it impossible for the researchers to move. If that does not sound like someone being held captive against their wishes, I don't know what does! Mugging has been documented worldwide in popular whale-watching areas in Australia (Hervey Bay), South Africa (Knysna), and Tonga. It is likely, not uncommon, within the whales' range and wherever they interact with boats.

While being mugged by a Humpback sounds like a pleasant experience to any whale lover, being mugged by an Orca, particularly when you are on a kayak feeling slightly vulnerable, sounds less relaxing. While apparently, and thankfully, not as common, close-up kayaking encounters have been reported in New Zealand and even California.

From whales to windmills

What better way to wrap up this chapter than to think about how Humpback Whales, the ballerinas of the ocean, with their ability to pirouette in tight circles while blowing bubbles (which allows them to corral prey for easy capture), actually move as they do? The tubercles, or small bumps, on the leading edge of their flippers have everything to do with it. Water moving over a smooth edge would break into a series of turbulent vortices as it passes over the flipper; the humpback tubercles maintain even channels of water flowing over, allowing increased "grip" on the water and enabling them to take tight turns. Replicating the tubercles on the blades of wind turbines decreased drag by 32 percent, increasing efficiency and power generation. While many interactions between humans and whales, intentional or unintentional, direct or indirect, end up in conflict, it is heartening to see how some individuals observe these species to innovate solutions in ways that would never be possible in their absence.

10

ECOLOGY AND CONSERVATION

THE INTERCONNECTEDNESS
OF SPECIES

Like all species, plant or animal, whales occupy a unique and important niche on our planet. As John Muir once said, "When we try to pick out anything by itself, we find it hitched to everything else in the universe," highlighting the interconnectedness of every species and ecosystem on our planet. Given this interconnectedness, the removal of any species through either the destruction of its habitat, the reduction or removal of its prey, or direct hunting can have devastating consequences.

Sea otters and ripple effects

This was very clearly demonstrated through the work done by Jim Estes on a marine mammal cousin of the whale, the sea otter population of the Aleutian Islands.

They extend across the North Pacific Ocean from Alaska to the coast of Kamchatka in Russia. Around two centuries ago, during the height of the fur trade, hunters descended on this corner of the globe in search of the most valuable and densest fur of all. The sea otter pelt has approximately 1 million hairs per square inch, making it highly desirable in the fur coat industry. Unfortunately, this desire for fur resulted in the Aleutian Island sea otters being driven almost to extinction by the 1900s. Thankfully, a swift decision to ban sea otter hunting came into place in 1911 through the International Fur Seal Treaty that saved this species. However, the impact of such extensive hunting was far-reaching and went beyond the decimation of sea otter populations.

As sea otter populations were driven down, sea urchins—their main prey—increased in both size and number. This resulted in the disappearance of entire kelp forests, which were replaced by sea urchins littering the barren seafloor. Bearing in mind that the kelp forests once provided nourishment and hiding

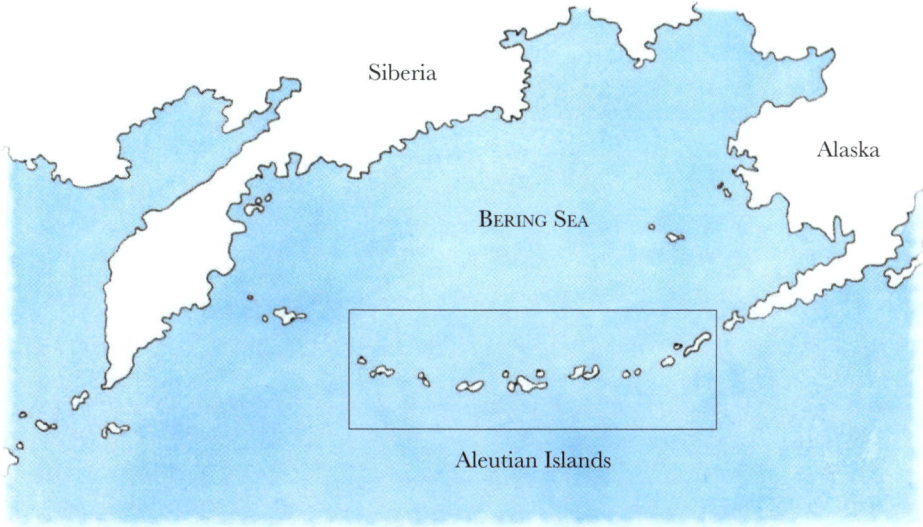

ALEUTIAN ISLANDS
This Pacific archipelago is one of the most remote places on Earth.

places for fish and other sea animals, their loss had further ripple effects throughout the ecosystem.

Nearby islands where sea otters had survived in greater numbers, or been reintroduced, provided evidence that this "trophic cascade" (the progression of indirect effects by predators across successively lower trophic levels) in the Aleutians was a direct result of the near eradication of the sea otter. What's more, it was not just an imbalance in the sea otters' own ecosystem, but the great reduction in their numbers that caused ripple effects far further afield. The loss of the kelp forests has damaged our ability to deal with rising carbon dioxide levels on our planet, because healthy kelp forests can absorb 4.91 megatons of carbon per year. The importance of this surely escapes no one in our increasingly warming world.

After nearly a century of recovery from overhunting, sea otter populations experienced another decline in western Alaska, which once again set off a trophic cascade. While sea otters are now protected from hunting, the cause is most likely linked with increased Orca predation. This in turn is linked to depleted stocks of the Orcas' traditional prey as a result of anthropogenic changes in the offshore oceanic system.

ALEUTIAN ISLAND SEA OTTERS
These intelligent creatures are one of the few non-human animals to use tools; they often carry a rock in their armpit pouch and use it to crack open hard-shelled prey like clams and mussels.

Sea otters are a keystone species, which means they have a disproportionately large effect on their environment relative to their biomass. Nonetheless, they are a great reminder to protect all species, because a lack of protection can lead to far-reaching and sometimes poorly understood ripple effects.

Whales as ecosystem engineers

Whales are often referred to as ecosystem engineers because, by definition, they are animals that create or modify their environment. They do this in two ways—through their feces and their rotting carcasses.

Whales dive to the depths to feed and, in these dark waters, their feasts include nutrients like iron and nitrogen that are limited in surface waters. After feeding they return to the surface where they often release plumes of fecal matter. Research in the Gulf of Maine has shown the important role of whales and other marine mammals in delivering increased amounts of nitrogen in the surface zone by feeding at depth and then pooing at the surface. This vertical movement of nutrients by whales is known as the "whale pump." This poo, spread across the surface waters, acts like fertilizer for tiny microscopic plants like phytoplankton. These phytoplankton feast on sunshine, as well as these nutrients and other things essential to the process of photosynthesis, and they release oxygen as a byproduct into the atmosphere. Fifty percent of all our planet's oxygen is produced in the ocean, and is mostly consumed by marine lifeforms that use it to keep our oceans alive. Phytoplankton also forms the base of all food webs in the ocean, so more of them means more of everything else. While poorly understood, the stimulation of phytoplankton growth and the sequestration of carbon dioxide in the process of photosynthesis further highlights the important role of whales in the ecosystem. One study found that a population of 12,000 Southern Ocean Sperm Whales (*Physeter macrocephalus*) indirectly draw 200,000 tons (180,000 tonnes) of carbon out of the atmosphere annually, simply by stimulating phytoplankton growth with their iron-rich feces.

Furthermore, baleen whales undertake some of the greatest annual

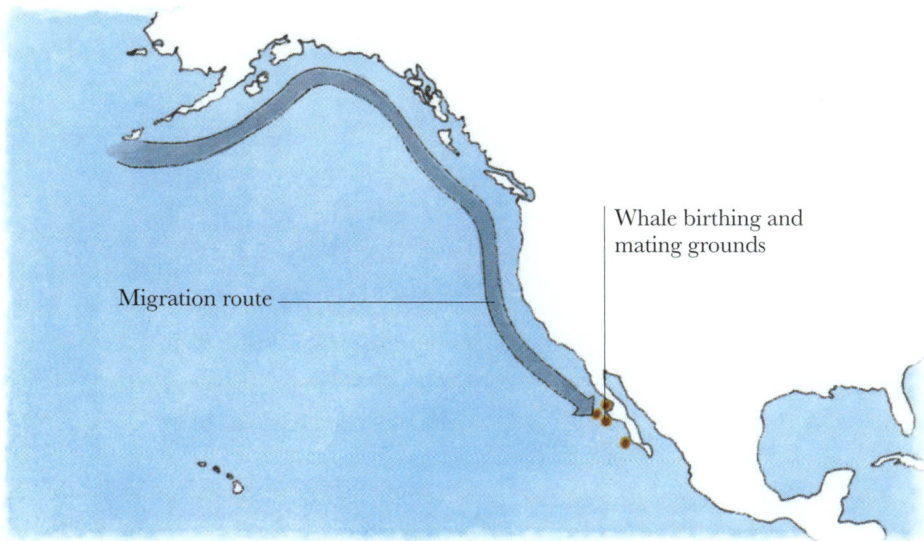

Whale birthing and mating grounds

Migration route

NORTH AMERICAN GRAY WHALE MIGRATION
This map shows the vast journey many Gray Whales undertake annually.

movements of all mammals with some of the longest migrations on the planet (see Chapter 6). Gray Whales (*Eschrichtius robustus*) off the west coast of North America travel nearly 10,000 miles (16,000 km) between their feeding and breeding grounds—and back again—over a seven-month period every year. During their travels,they transport nutrients from the productive feeding areas to the less productive but warmer calving areas thousands of miles away. Nutrients released on the breeding grounds are seen as new nutrients to the system, thus stimulating new primary production, carbon export, and carbon sequestration. Nutrients released on the feeding grounds stimulate both recycled primary production and carbon export. In this way, whales have an uncanny ability to carry nutrients from places that have it to places that need it.

Apart from spreading essential nutrients throughout the ocean with their feces, whales are also vital to the ecosystem in their death. Their carcasses, also known as "whale fall," are the largest form of detritus to fall from the surface to the seafloor. As some of the longest-lived animals on the planet, they constitute one of the largest stable living carbon pools in the ocean. As the dead whales descend, they provide pulses of enrichment in a generally food-poor environment. They provide a meal to some 400 species that are well adapted to these extreme conditions, such as the eel-shaped, slime-producing hagfish that lurks at the darkest depths.

During the two hundred years when industrialized whaling was widespread, the killing of whales and subsequent removal of their carcasses inevitably altered the rates and geographic distribution of whale falls to the deep-sea floor, leading to the extinction of species that were most specialized and reliant on the carcasses for their survival. The immense impact of this is difficult to comprehend. As the carcasses of certain baleen whales, including Blue (*Balaenoptera musculus*), Humpback (*Megaptera novaeangliae*), and Minke (*B. acutorostrata*) Whales, drop to the bottom, they are thought to transfer about 30,000 tons (27,200 tonnes) of carbon per year from the atmosphere to deeper waters. These waters act as carbon sinks—places in the environment that delay or prevent global warming by absorbing, storing, or holding carbon from the atmosphere for hundreds to thousands of years. If great whale populations were to rebound to their pre-commercial whaling size, this carbon sink could increase five-fold.

The financial value of a whale

Based on the many benefits great whales provide, including their robust capacity for capturing carbon, researchers at the International Monetary Fund have calculated that each great whale alive today is worth $2 million, totalling $1 trillion for the current total global "stock." While the details of these calculations remain debated, and leave me wondering why we can only entice people to protect these giants if there is a dollar value on their head, economists suggest we use this to argue that if we protect great whales, they will continue to provide us with a plethora of services that are worth a lot of money and it will reap major dividends for the planet.

THREATS TO WHALES

Whales are the largest animals on Earth, but their size does not always protect them from the many threats they face. Whales are a K-selected species, which means they produce few offspring but invest lots of energy in them, with a long gestation period, long-lasting parental care, and an extended period until the sexual maturity of calves. They produce offspring that each have a relatively good chance of survival to maturity. K-selection is more typical of larger species like whales and elephants, which have longer lifespans, overlapping generations, and altricial young that are born helpless and require extensive care from adults. These characteristics, which result in slow population increases, are precisely why K-selected species are more vulnerable to extinction. Indeed, six of the thirteen great whale species are today classified as threatened or vulnerable.

Vessel collisions

Thousands of whales are either injured or killed in collisions with ships every year. Given that shipping is the most efficient means of transporting traded goods the world over, we can only expect an increase in ships with time. Ship-strikes, or vessel collisions, are now the leading cause of death for large whale species worldwide.

Vessel collisions impact all large whale species, including Blue, Fin (*B. physalus*), Sei (*B. borealis*), Bryde's (*B. edeni*), Humpback, Right (*Eubalaena glacialis*), Gray, and Sperm Whales. Whale carcasses often become wrapped across container ships bows, only to be discovered on arrival in port. While whales are the largest animals on our planet, they are no match for ships that can be more than 1,000 times as heavy as the largest Blue Whale. Interactions that happen at speed are particularly lethal, leaving the whales with little time to escape.

Global ship traffic overlaps with the ranges of almost all whale species, and most of these areas have very few protections in place. Protections might include rerouting ships out of certain areas, creating alert systems that can warn authorities or mariners about nearby whales, and mandatory speed reductions. Speed reductions have additional benefits such as reducing underwater noise pollution, greenhouse gas emissions, and air pollution, all of which benefit coastal communities.

Entanglement and bycatch

Approximately 300,000 whales, dolphins, and porpoises are killed because of entanglements with fishing gear every year. Growing shipping is leading to more collisions between whales and ships, and with the increase in ships comes an increase in ocean noise pollution. Climate change is also causing shifts in prey, sometimes leading whales to move into less protected areas.

The entanglement and accidental catch (bycatch) of whales in fishing gear poses a significant threat to a range of species. Entanglement in fishing gear such as gill nets, long lines, and discarded trawl nets may lead to mortality either directly, through drowning, or indirectly, via impaired locomotion or foraging efficiency.

Gill net entanglements impact both the smallest and the largest cetaceans (the Vaquita (*Phocoena sinus*) and the Blue Whale) on our planet. While mortality reports for Blue Whales are low, this could be because of "cryptic bycatch." Cryptic bycatch is not recorded in fisheries statistics because some whales, particularly the larger ones that get caught in fishing gear, swim away injured or subsequently die, with or without gear attached. As a result, the overall impact of entanglement is unknown and varies between populations depending on their demography, population size, and bycatch rate.

Microplastics

Microplastics form when larger plastic objects in the ocean break down due to wind, wave motion, and heat from the sun. Whales predominantly feed 165–820 ft (50–250 m) below the surface, a depth that unfortunately coincides with the highest concentrations of microplastics in the ocean. Blue Whales are said to ingest an estimated 10 million pieces of microplastic per day. The simple food chain of a Blue Whale—the krill eats the plastic and the whale eats the

BLUE WHALE FEEDING
It is thought that Blue Whales unknowingly ingest around 10 million pieces of microplastic every single day.

krill—leads to this particularly high concentration. Species that feed higher up the food chain, like Humpback Whales that feed on fish, can still eat 200,000 pieces per day, however. Fin Whales that feed on both fish and krill ingest between 3 and 10 million pieces per day.

Given the prevalence of microplastics in our ocean, one might assume that whales consume so many microplastics because they gulp down such large amounts of seawater. In fact, microplastics mostly come from prey. We do not have a definitive answer on whether microplastics in the belly of krill reduce the nutritional value to a whale, whether microplastics scratch a whale's stomach lining, or whether they are absorbed into the whale's bloodstream. So much on this subject is still unknown.

Ocean noise

Animals in the ocean rely on sound for many things—in fact, their very survival depends on their ability to hear. Sound is an essential means of communication underwater and the primary means by which many marine species gather and understand information about their environment. They use it to find prey, communicate with one another, find mates and offspring, avoid predators, keep their social groups together, and navigate.

A great range of sounds are generated in the ocean, and their sources vary. Abiotic sounds are made by wind, waves, rain, or earthquakes. The ocean's inhabitants, such as marine mammals and fish, produce biotic sounds, and anthropogenic sounds are those that are produced by or the result of us humans. Not all of these are classed as noise, because ocean noise is specifically sound made by human activities that can interfere with or obscure the ability of marine animals to hear natural sounds in the ocean. Thus noise is any sound that negatively impacts marine life.

Over the last century, human activities such as recreational boating, shipping, and oil and gas exploration have increased along our coastlines, as well as offshore and in deep-sea environments. Noise from these activities can travel long distances underwater, altering our coastal and offshore habitats in ways we are still trying to comprehend.

As noise in the ocean increases, many essential functions get disrupted, negatively impacting marine species and ecosystems. Higher noise levels can reduce the ability of animals to communicate with potential mates, other group members, or even their own offspring. Noise can also reduce their ability to hear environmental cues vital for their survival, including those key to avoiding predators, finding mates, locating food and other dangers, and navigating to preferred habitats.

Climate change

Climate change can affect the distribution, timing, and range of migration, the abundance of competitors and predators, the availability of prey, the timing of breeding, and reproductive success. As our oceans warm, environments change, and species have few options. They can adapt to the warming temperature, learn to tolerate it, or move—if not, they risk extinction. If temperatures change gradually, adaptation and increasing tolerance are possible. However, our world is warming at an alarming rate. Temperatures are increasing so rapidly that gradual adaptation or tolerance are rarely possible. The option of moving to escape rising temperatures exists and, in the ocean, we expect species to move deeper or to higher latitudes (as the oceans are warming poleward). This means species from the tropics are predicted to move toward polar and temperate waters. But the movement is not straightforward. Not only will species have to move into unknown habitats, bringing them face to face with species that already live there—leading to potential competition or replacement—but they may face new and perhaps even bigger threats. Resident species tied to specific ocean basins, such as Northern Indian Ocean Blue Whales and Arabian Sea Humpback Whales, will likely be left with nowhere to go as they get trapped in their ecological cul-de-sacs.

Climate change is also causing shifts to seasonal ice coverage and thickness, affecting the migration of Belugas (*Delphinapterus leucas*) and increasing their potential to become trapped in ice. This could reduce their ability to find prey and make them more vulnerable to predators, or the ice may prevent them from coming to the surface to breathe, leading to suffocation. The Arctic is warming four times faster than the global average. As the sea ice melts (predicted to vanish completely by 2035), it opens up new trans-Arctic shipping routes

CHINOOK SALMON
*The Chinook is the largest species of Pacific salmon, with
some individuals reaching 5 ft (1.5 m) in length.*

by expanding areas of navigable water. This leads to an increased risk of collision between Bowhead Whales and ships (called ship-strike) and increased
impacts from noise pollution. Warming oceans can also disrupt whale migrations as prey abundance and distribution changes in response—for example, it
heavily impacts the Chinook salmon population and their migratory routes.
Their declining numbers are bad news for their predators, the endangered
southern resident Orcas (*Orcinus orca*).

Tourism

Tourism is often touted as a tool for positive change, but it must be managed with
care, foresight, and a genuine commitment to sustainability. While long-term
impacts are hard to ascertain, as whale-related tourism is a relatively new industry, there is concern that continued close approaches by whale-watching boats or
swimmers attempting to get a closer view may disrupt the normal behavior patterns of whales or drive them away from preferred habitats and prey. This can
impact the whales' long-term health, preventing them from feeding adequately
and reducing their energy budgets (on which capital breeders like large whales
depend), delaying or halting reproduction, causing loss of feeding opportunities,
increasing stress levels, and reducing their capacity to detect mates or predators.

SPECIES AT RISK OR LOST

We often believe that charismatic megafauna, like whales, have a higher chance of survival by virtue of their physical size and ability to capture the hearts and minds of even the youngest among us. Unfortunately, this assumption does not hold true for a number of cetacean species that come into direct conflict with human needs and wants. This often leaves me wondering, if we cannot save even these admired and popular species, what chance do we have of saving those generally considered less charismatic?

Two species that have captured our attention because of their consistently dwindling numbers are the Vaquita and the North Atlantic Right Whale. While Vaquitas are the smallest cetaceans, North Atlantic Right Whales are large, but what they have in common is the key threat that they face: fishing. One is as bycatch to an illegal fishery, while the other is impacted by entanglement in a long-standing traditional fishery.

Vaquita

The Vaquita is the smallest cetacean in our oceans, measuring about 5 ft (1.5 m) on average. Yet, it has made big news by becoming the most endangered cetacean in the world. The name Vaquita means little cow, while its scientific name, *Phocoena sinus*, means porpoise of the Gulf. Vaquitas lack a beak, have a smiling upturned mouth and black rings around their eyes, and are mostly dark gray with lighter gray undersides. Unusually, their triangular dorsal fins in the middle of their backs are taller and wider than that of most other porpoises.

These little marine mammals are found exclusively in the shallow waters of the northern Gulf of California, Mexico, and, unfortunately, their restricted range makes them particularly vulnerable. The gulf is home to several fisheries, including an illegal one for totoaba, a large and critically endangered fish endemic to the region. The totoaba is prized for its swim bladder, also known as "maw." This gas-filled sac helps bony fish maintain

VAQUITA
The Vaquita is both the smallest and the most endangered cetacean globally.

and control their buoyancy and is a delicacy in China, where it is used in traditional medicines and cosmetics. As a result of the expanding demand for these swim bladders, which fetch thousands of dollars per pound on the Chinese black market, fishers and poachers use gillnets, which are officially banned in Vaquita habitats, and which sadly also pull up the endemic Vaquita. This uncontrolled and illegal exploitation of totoaba swim bladder has resulted in the decline of the Vaquita population to fewer than ten individuals at the last count—a devastating 99 percent decline in the last decade.

Despite both the Vaquita and the totoaba being protected under Appendix I of the Convention on International Trade in Endangered Species of Wild Fauna and Flora (CITES), which bans their commercial trade, there has been an increase in the presence of totoaba online, suggesting that the demand in China has not waned and likely will not any time soon. The high prices paid on the black market for totoaba swim bladders far outpace what local fishers make in a legal fishery, earning the fish the moniker "the cocaine of the sea." Unfortunately, the lack of governance to enforce another way of fishing, and support and compensate fishers who fish in a way that would allow Vaquita to survive, means the future does not look bright for this species.

North Atlantic Right Whale

Nine times as long as the Vaquita, at 45 ft (14 m), North Atlantic Right Whales are also, unfortunately, a critically endangered species as of 2020. With a population of fewer than 400 and fewer than 100 reproductively active females, scientists have been monitoring this population closely for years. They are sadly dying at a rate faster than they can reproduce, with females producing fewer calves each year. Female Right Whales become sexually mature at age ten and are pregnant for a year, giving birth to a single calf. Previously, they produced a calf every three years, but this calving interval has now increased to six to ten years, potentially because of increased stress from entanglements, vessel strikes, and climate change-driven shifts in prey availability. In 2024, 20 calves were born, which might sound like cause for celebration. However, given the high rate of human-caused mortality and serious injury, 50 or more newborns are needed annually to stop the population decline and allow for recovery.

Since 2017, due to a spike in deaths, these whales have been experiencing what scientists call an unusual mortality event (UME). Under the U.S. Marine Mammal Protection Act, given that these whales primarily occur in Atlantic

NORTH ATLANTIC RIGHT WHALE
These whales have unique raised patches of skin on their heads. These form distinct patterns, allowing researchers to identify individuals much as we would use fingerprints to identify individual humans.

coastal waters on the continental shelf, a UME is "a stranding that is unexpected; involves a significant die-off of any marine mammal population; and demands immediate response." The primary causes of the UME are entanglements in fishing gear and collisions with boats and ships.

Scientists estimate that over 85 percent of Right Whales have been entangled in fishing gear at least once. Even if the whale eventually becomes free, the time spent entangled can elevate stress levels and have other impacts, including preventing it from feeding, and diverting energy from more important activities such as swimming, feeding, and reproducing. The gear can also cut into their bodies, leading to injury and potentially delayed mortality. Unfortunately, the range of this species overlaps with major ports along the Atlantic coastline, as well as with shipping lanes. This increases the Right Whales' vulnerability to vessel collision, which can result in broken bones, internal injuries, cuts, or death.

Other potential drivers of population decline include climate change and ocean noise. Over the last decade, scientists have noted a shift in the distribution of Right Whales. These shifts are typically in response to changes in prey location and availability in the face of warming oceans. This change has meant that whales are now spending more time in areas where they are more vulnerable to vessel strikes and entanglements and are afforded less protection. Ocean noise can interrupt behavior, interfere with communication, and reduce their ability to detect and avoid predators, find food, and find mates.

LOST ON OUR WATCH

The Baiji, or Chinese River Dolphin (*Lipotes vexillifer*) has the unfortunate distinction of being the first dolphin declared extinct in modern times. It also represents the first global extinction of a megafaunal vertebrate for over 50

CHINESE RIVER DOLPHIN
Sadly this species is now lost forever.

years and the disappearance of an entire mammal family, the Lipotidae. A river dolphin that once roamed the Yangtze River, it experienced a precipitous decline between 1980 and 1997–1999, when its population dropped from 400 to just 13 individuals. The last verified reports of Baiji were of a pregnant female stranded at Zhenjiang in November 2001 and an individual photographed in the Tongling River in May 2002. Sadly, an intensive six-week multi-vessel visual and acoustic survey in 2006 failed to find any evidence of the species alive. The demise of this dolphin has been deemed "a national tragedy for China and an international disgrace" and is, again, the result of harmful fishing practices such as rolling hook long-lines and habitat degradation. Clearly, while these species are all considered charismatic, this alone could not save them.

"SAVE THE WHALE" IS SELLING US SHORT

There was a time when our oceans were teeming with whales. In the 1600s whalers "joked" that there were enough Right Whales in Cape Cod bay off the East Coast of the United States that it was possible to walk across their backs from one end of the bay to the next. Today there are fewer than 400 of these whales left, and they are critically endangered.

The Save the Whales movement of the 1970s was instrumental in halting commercial whaling. Environmental and animal rights organizations worked hard to expose the cruelty inflicted and fought for the sake of biodiversity. Their success was reflected in the global moratorium on commercial whaling put in place in the early 1980s. Nonetheless, over the last two decades most whale populations around the world have struggled to recover their numbers. While some countries still indulge in whaling in violation of the moratorium or in the name of science, this is not the main reason population numbers are low.

Activists often ask me for money to "save the whales." Given that my biggest mission in life is encompassed by that phrase, I ask them, "Why?" It turns out that the compelling story of whales being slaughtered for their meat still tugs at heart-strings and is a means by which these advocacy groups raise funds. Many believe the whales should be saved because they are charismatic megafauna, and yet answers of this nature are a disservice to these magnificent ocean giants. As we have seen, the presence of whales in our oceans is critical for ocean resilience because whales are not just pretty faces; they are ecosystem engineers. They maintain the health and stability of the oceans; they are also beneficial to human society.

Countless reports tell us we have done the unthinkable by reducing population sizes of various vertebrate species so drastically in recent generations. It makes one wonder—what can we do? I believe that we are selling charismatic megafauna short by not contextualizing our conservation messages. As conservationists, we should be creating awareness about the true ecosystem value of these species so people understand the real importance of protecting these giants—because of their essential ecosystem functions, as well as for their acrobatics and grace. Saving whales should not be focused on whaling, because that is only part of the problem and there are more pressing modern issues faced by whale populations.

Since 90 percent of all transported human goods are shipped, we are all guilty of killing whales. The container ships that move our food and clothes from one part of the globe to the other are killing whales; our fishing nets are drowning whales, and our search for oil and gas is deafening them and driving them out of areas that are integral to their safety. Using outdated campaigns does more damage than good because the true causes of death go unnoticed. It enables people to point fingers at others rather than forcing them to take responsibility for their own part in the destruction. Let's save the whales, certainly, but by revising and updating the old campaigns to make a real difference for the oceans.

Over the last few decades, we have seriously grown our knowledge about cetaceans, their habitats, and their habits. There is plenty more we need to learn, but for now, we have enough to tell us that we should be doing better and we should be designing better systems that "whale-safe" our oceans.

Ways to improve

Off southern Sri Lanka, shipping companies are voluntarily moving offshore, out of whale hotspots, to prevent collisions with Blue Whales and Bryde's Whales, while off Panama, commercial shipping lanes have been officially moved to benefit Humpback Whales. With the understanding that slower vessels are less likely to be involved in lethal collisions, Panama has also asked vessels to slow down, a measure also in place in the Santa Barbara channel off California. An added benefit of slow downs is the reduced release of greenhouse gases, making this a win-win decision. Off British Columbia, Canada, mariners receive an alert if whales are in the area, enabling vessels to undertake adaptive mitigation measures, such as slowing down or altering course in the presence of whales, to reduce the risk of collision and disturbance. Some of these alert systems rely on citizen or community scientists to report sightings that are then relayed to the mariners—enabling many people to participate in solving the problem of ship-strikes.

Scientists are working alongside fishers to develop ways to avoid whale/gear entanglements. Ropeless systems eliminate the risk of entanglement by removing the vertical lines that attach surface buoys to pots and traps. Acoustic deterrent devices or pingers that emit pulses of high-frequency sound to deter cetaceans from approaching fishing gear have successfully reduced marine mammal bycatch in the California drift gillnet fishery. While the pingers are often put in place to stop the cetaceans from entangling in nets, pingers are currently being trialed off Portugal to deter Orcas from making contact with yachts.

Many other efforts are in place to reduce threats that affect whale populations, and while none of these systems are perfect, they underline the capacity of humans to be part of the solution and not just part of the problem.

LIST OF SPECIES

Baleen whales

Balaena mysticetus (Bowhead Whale, Greenland Whale)

Balaenoptera acutorostrata (Common Minke Whale)

Balaenoptera bonaerensis (Antarctic Minke Whale)

Balaenoptera borealis (Sei Whale)

Balaenoptera edeni (Bryde's Whale)

Balaenoptera musculus (Blue Whale)

Balaenoptera omurai (Omura's Whale)

Balaenoptera physalus (Fin Whale)

Balaenoptera ricei (Rice's Whale)

Caperea marginata (Pygmy Right Whale)

Eschrichtius robustus (Gray Whale)

Eubalaena australis (Southern Right Whale)

Eubalaena glacialis (North Atlantic Right Whale)

Eubalaena japonica (North Pacific Right Whale)

Megaptera novaeangliae (Humpback Whale)

Toothed whales

Berardius arnuxii (Arnoux's Beaked Whale)

Berardius bairdii (Baird's Beaked Whale)

Berardius minimus (Sato's Beaked Whale)

Cephalorhynchus commersonii (Commerson's Dolphin)

Cephalorhynchus eutropia (Chilean Dolphin)

Cephalorhynchus heavisidii (Heaviside's Dolphin)

Cephalorhynchus hectori (Hector's Dolphin)

Delphinapterus leucas (Beluga, White Whale)

Delphinus delphis (Common Dolphin)

Feresa attenuata (Pygmy Killer Whale)

Globicephala macrorhynchus (Short-finned Pilot Whale)

Globicephala melas (Long-finned Pilot Whale)

Grampus griseus (Risso's Dolphin, Grampus)

Hyperoodon ampullatus (Northern Bottlenose Whale)

Hyperoodon planifrons (Southern Bottlenose Whale)

Indopacetus pacificus (Longman's Beaked Whale, Tropical Bottlenose Whale)

Inia geoffrensis (Amazon River Dolphin)

Kogia breviceps (Pygmy Sperm Whale)

Kogia sima (Dwarf Sperm Whale)

Lagenodelphis hosei (Fraser's Dolphin)

Lagenorhynchus acutus (Atlantic White-sided Dolphin)

Lagenorhynchus albirostris (White-beaked Dolphin)

Lagenorhynchus australis (Peale's Dolphin)

Lagenorhynchus cruciger (Hourglass Dolphin)

Lagenorhynchus obliquidens (Pacific White-sided Dolphin)

Lagenorhynchus obscurus (Dusky Dolphin)

Lipotes vexillifer (Baiji, Yangtze River Dolphin)—possibly extinct

Lissodelphis borealis (Northern Right-whale Dolphin)

Lissodelphis peronii (Southern Right-whale Dolphin)

Mesoplodon bidens (Sowerby's Beaked Whale)

Mesoplodon bowdoini (Andrews' Beaked Whale)

Mesoplodon carlhubbsi (Hubbs' Beaked Whale)

Mesoplodon densirostris (Blainville's Beaked Whale)

Mesoplodon eueu (Ramari's Beaked Whale)

Mesoplodon europaeus (Gervais' Beaked Whale)

Mesoplodon ginkgodens (Ginkgo-toothed Beaked Whale)

Mesoplodon grayi (Gray's Beaked Whale)

Mesoplodon hectori (Hector's Beaked Whale)

Mesoplodon hotaula (Deraniyagala's Beaked Whale)

Mesoplodon layardii (Strap-toothed Beaked Whale, Layard's Beaked Whale)

Mesoplodon mirus (True's Beaked Whale)

Mesoplodon perrini (Perrin's Beaked Whale)

Mesoplodon peruvianus (Pygmy Beaked Whale)

Mesoplodon stejnegeri (Stejneger's Beaked Whale)

Mesoplodon traversii (Spade-toothed Whale)

Monodon monoceros (Narwhal)

Neophocaena asiaeorientalis (Narrow-ridged Finless Porpoise)

Neophocaena phocaenoides (Indo-Pacific Finless Porpoise)

Orcaella brevirostris (Irrawaddy Dolphin, Pesut)

Orcaella heinsohni (Australian Snubfin Dolphin)

Orcinus orca (Killer Whale, Orca)

Peponocephala electra (Melon-headed Whale)

Phocoena dioptrica (Spectacled Porpoise)

Phocoena phocoena (Harbor Porpoise)

Phocoena sinus (Vaquita)

Phocoena spinipinnis (Burmeister's Porpoise)

Phocoenoides dalli (Dall's Porpoise)

Physeter macrocephalus (Sperm Whale, Cachalot)

Platanista gangetica (Ganges River Dolphin, Susu)

Platanista minor (Indus River Dolphin, Bhulan)

Pontoporia blainvillei (Franciscana, Toninha)

Pseudorca crassidens (False Killer Whale)

Sotalia fluviatilis (Tucuxi)

Sotalia guianensis (Guiana Dolphin, Costero)

Sousa chinensis (Indo-Pacific Humpback Dolphin)

Sousa plumbea (Indian Ocean Humpback Dolphin)

Sousa sahulensis (Australian Humpback Dolphin)

Sousa teuszii (Atlantic Humpback Dolphin)

Stenella attenuata (Pantropical Spotted Dolphin)

Stenella clymene (Clymene Dolphin)

Stenella coeruleoalba (Striped Dolphin)

Stenella frontalis (Atlantic Spotted Dolphin)

Stenella longirostris (Spinner Dolphin)

Steno bredanensis (Rough-toothed Dolphin)

Tasmacetus shepherdi (Shepherd's Beaked Whale, Tasman Beaked Whale)

Tursiops aduncus (Indo-Pacific Bottlenose Dolphin)

Tursiops erebennus (Tamanend's Bottlenose Dolphin)

Tursiops truncatus (Common Bottlenose Dolphin)

Ziphius cavirostris (Cuvier's Beaked Whale, Goose-beaked Whale)

For more information, see the Committee on Taxonomy of the Society of Marine Mammalogy https://marinemammalscience. org/science-and-publications/ list-marine-mammal-species- subspecies

INDEX

ACKNOWLEDGMENTS

This book exists because of all the people who rallied around me on this very long journey: my lecturers, who enthusiastically shared their knowledge and wisdom about whales in my formative years as a marine mammal science student; my friends in the marine mammal community, too many to name, whose research has excited me so much that the opportunity to write about it in these pages was unmissable.

Adrian Sington, my agent, negotiator, and protector at Kruger Cowne, thank you. It's always a fun ride with you—may there be many more projects in our collective future. To the publishing team at UniPress and Princeton, who scoured the world and chose my voice to carry the stories of these incredible beasts, specifically Jason Hook and Robert Kirk. To my commissioning editor, Claire Collins, for her patience and gentle nudging that kept things and me on the straight and narrow, and to Paul Palmer-Edwards, my book designer, who has masterfully matched visual appeal and intellectual appeal in these pages. Adam Hook for taking us back to the wonderful days of illustrated books, and Robert Brandt, who created the infographics and maps. To Rob Young at Coastal Carolina University, my peer reviewer, who scoured through these pages with a fine-toothed comb, and while I am grateful you did not have much to do, the comments you made were significant—thank you.

To Niam, who appeared on the planet and immediately became one of the most important drivers for me to do what I do. Who will probably not understand how much he means to me right now, but hopefully will, someday soon. To Aiaa my brother, for drawing two very accurate dolphins in the background of my less accurate depiction of whales in my "Save Our Sea Mammals" poster when I was six—thus unknowingly supporting what was to come. To Charith, thank you for remaining zen even as I tornado around you and for letting me find my balance between all the things I passionately throw myself into and attempt to juggle. To Amma and Thaththa, my parents, this book is dedicated to you because it would not exist without me, and I would not exist without you.

To those who told me I could not, would not, and was not enough to succeed as a marine mammal scientist—I hope you all have the pleasure of reading this book. Your naysaying fueled me into realms I may not have reached otherwise. To all of you who see yourselves in me, I hope you realize this book is not just a book about whales, but in some ways, it's an indication of what is possible for all of us—no matter who we are, where we come from, or how the past saw us. If I can, you can.